Ghost Towns of Montana

Ghost Towns of Montana

by Don C. Miller

PRUETT PUBLISHING COMPANY
BOULDER, COLORADO

Paperback Edition, First Printing: 1981

9

Printed in the United States of America

Library of Congress Catalog Card Number: 72-95496
ISBN: 0-87108-606-9

To Sue

PREFACE

It was there for the taking—mostly the gold nuggets and dust, but also the copper, molybdenum, cinnabar, and precious silver.

So men panned creeks and burrowed into mountains. They built rockers and arrastres. Miners, like moles and prairie dogs, sank prospect holes. "Hydraulic giants" hammered streams of water against bars, benches and ledges to pound away the soil and expose the gold. Dredges clawed the stream beds. Sluice boxes collected gold. Stamp mills dotted the landscape. Blasting caps, dynamite, cyanide and quicksilver became more common than bacon and eggs.

Fortunes were made easily and lost easily in California and Oregon, in Nevada, Utah and South Dakota, in Washington and Alaska, and along the Rockies in Montana, Idaho, Wyoming, Colorado, New Mexico and Arizona.

Some miners went it alone. Many formed partnerships. Some worked for mining companies.

Most worked hard, and played hard. A few claims were jumped, but not many. There was even a Miner's Ten Commandments to guide conduct, drawn up in Bannack, Montana. They ordered:

FIRST COMMANDMENT: Thou shalt have no other claim than one.

SECOND COMMANDMENT: Thou shalt not make thyself any false claims or any likeness to a mean man, by jumping one; for I, a miner, am a just man and I will visit the miners round about and they will judge thee; and when they shall decide thou wilt take thy pick thy pan thy shovel and thy blankets and with all thou hast thou shalt depart to seek other diggings but thou shalt find none.

THIRD COMMANDMENT: Thou shalt not go prospecting before thy claim gives out. Neither shalt thou take thy money or gold dust or thy good name to the gaming table for monte twenty-one roulette faro lunsquent and poker will prove thee that the more thou puttest down the less thou shalt take up and when thou thinkest of thy wife and children thou shalt hold thyself guiltless though insane.

FOURTH COMMANDMENT: Thou shalt keep the Sabbath day holy and shall do no work other than cooking the pork and beans for the week's supply getting in firewood and doing the week's wash and baking the week's supply of bread.

(The fifth commandment is skipped, presumably because the Biblical command is accepted without revision.)

SIXTH COMMANDMENT: Thou shalt not drink mint juleps nor sherry cobblers through a straw nor gurgle from a bottle the raw materials nor take it from a decanter; for while thou are swallowing down thy purse and the coat from thy back thou art burning the coat off thy stomach.

SEVENTH COMMANDMENT: Thou shalt not grow discouraged and think of going home before thou hast made thy pile because thou hast not struck a lead, nor found a rich crevice nor sunk a shaft upon a rich pocket, lest in going home thou shalt leave a job paying four dollars a day to take, ashamed, a job back east at 50 cents a day; and serve thee right. Thou knowest that by staying here thou mightest strike a lead and make 50 dollars a day and keep thy self-respect and when thou goest home thou shalt have enough to make thyself and others happy.

EIGHTH COMMANDMENT: Thou shalt not steal the dust or the tools of another miner, for he will surely find out what thou hast done and will call together his fellow miners and they, unless the law hinders them, will hand thee or give thee fifty lashes, or shave thy head or brand thy cheek with an "R" like a horse, to be read by all men.

NINTH COMMANDMENT: Thou shalt tell no false tales about good diggins in the mountains, to benefit a friend who may have mules, blankets or provisions and tools that he wishes to sell lest thy neighbor, deceived by thee into making the trip shall one day return through the snow with naught left but his rifle, contents of which he shall present to you in a manner that shall cause thee to fall down and die like a dog.

TENTH COMMANDMENT: Remember thy wife and children that are in the east and be true to them in thought, word and deed. Avoid the temptation to become a squaw-man and to people this country with half-breeds, for while there is naught to be said against these boys and girls as individuals, the fact remains that they will give the Indians the benefit of their white training and thus make the redskins more dangerous to the white man.[1]

The price of gold fluctuated before it was standardized at $32.00 per troy ounce in 1934. But usually the price was good.

Archimedes Principle? Few had heard of it, but they all applied it. Tell a miner the specific gravity of water is one, that of typical rocks 2.5 and that of gold 19.3; he cared not. He simply knew the gold was heavier than anything else. It sank to the bottom of the sluice box or the gold pan, and it bought the things he needed like a can of beans at $5.00. In April, 1865, in Virginia City, Montana, the asking price of flour was $110 per hundred. But at a place like Cable where a single nugget, supposedly the world's largest,[2] assayed at $19,000, such prices could easily be met.

The year 1907 was a turning point for many miners. A mining panic resulted from an 1893 act of congress which killed the Silver Act. Prices of precious metals fell. Claims petered out. For a while, large, mechanized operations were the only profitable ones . . . then they too were abandoned.

The miners left. Some scurried away so fast they left cooking utensils on still-warm stoves, and eating utensils on the rough-hewn wooden tables.

Many tried to wait it out, certain that things had to get better. But when?

One by one the holdouts left, for there were no reasons to stay, and many reasons to leave.

1. *Dillon Examiner,* September 20, 1939.

2. The nugget is reported to have been on display at the World's Fair. An eyewitness says the nugget covered the open pages of an unabridged dictionary.

Where there had once been raucous noises in crowded saloons, the rasp of shovel in rock, the scraping of the gold pans, there now is silence. Ultimately even the pack rats left; there was nothing left for them to steal.

Sun and wind and snow ravaged the false-fronted business places. Whip-sawed, mud-chinked cabins crumbled into the weeds. Wooden handles rotted from shovels. Hinges rusted and creaked and lost their grip and let their doors fall away. Nails withered in rotten wood. Roofs buckled and buildings swayed and collapsed.

Today vestiges of this era in American history remain—more in the Southwest, where the weather is kinder, but much even in the harsh Northwest.

The history buff, the photographer, the bottle collector can still find memorabilia.

No state has been more negligent in preserving these remarkable sites than Montana, where gold dust first was found in 1852.[3]

This is the sometimes romanticized story of what is and something of what was of the few extant Montana ghost towns.

Much of the history of the ghost towns is interred with its citizens. The grave markers tell a part of this tale. So do memories of the living and the dead.

The mood of the ghost town visitor affects what he senses. Personality, weather, attitudes of the people met, preconceptions of what the ghost towner expected to see, all affect reactions. For many the most interesting aspects of visiting a ghost town is their imagination. Did a Chinaman live here because the cabin is so small? What type music did they dance to at the Miner's Union Hall? Was the bank ever robbed? Was anyone hanged from that tree? What did the girl under this grave marker die of, when she was only three months old? Was the gold really down at the grass roots along this creek? Did they really bury a bottle of champagne with prostitutes?

For a moment at least, life can return to a ghost town in the form of a question, a reflection, a mystery.

What's left of these towns tells much of the American West; the good and the bad, the strong and the weak, the admirable and the contemptible.

These are facts and fairy tales selected roughly a century after it all began, of places and people from an era too long ago to be remembered, but recent enough to be recalled.

3. Personal letter from K. Ross Toole, University of Montana history professor.

ACKNOWLEDGMENTS

All inaccuracies in this book are those of the author.

The January 26, 1889 edition of the *Montana Livestock Journal* reported "Born . . . to Mr. and Mrs. Man-That-Carries-His-Gun-With-Him, a son, weighing 27 pounds and 10 ounces. This may seem a very large child, but it must be borne in mind that it is a large reservation." As a parallel, it should also be borne in mind that this partial history of Montana ghost towns and mining camps represents an effort toward an understanding of, and appreciation for, pioneer efforts to bring to fruition big dreams in the "Big Sky" country.

Without the help of the following, this book would never have been written:

Warren J. Brier, dean of the University of Montana School of Journalism, who suggested such a project be undertaken.

Muriel Sibell Wolle, whose pioneer efforts in the field will certainly stand for years as an historical-artistic-literary landmark.

Librarians at the University of Montana and the Montana Historical Society.

Bob McGiffert, professor of journalism at the University of Montana, who spent long hours applying his editing pencil to the manuscript.

Deane Jones, columnist for the Missoula *Missoulian*, who assisted in encouraging his readership to submit photos and information on various mining camps.

Gypo, the black lab—our protector during numerous camping expeditions in search of information and photographs—who flushed out much interesting Montana wildlife from the mountains, valleys and meadows we visited.

Daughter Shari, who being closer to terra firma than we, spotted many things we would have missed.

Sue, who with her quick eye and gregariousness, found interesting objects, and ferreted out many facts and personal recollections.

The University of Montana for providing financial support for travel and research.

And finally, to many Montana informants, who would appear to have an unflagging interest in and extensive knowledge of ghost towns—a meaningful and irreplaceable part of their heritage.

All photos not otherwise credited are by the author

CONTENTS

ARGENTA: Its silver dollars reportedly paled the fame of Golconda and El Dorado.

Probably Argenta is the second oldest quartz camp in Montana.[1] Here, too, is located the Legal Tender, the first silver-lead mine in the state. As late as 1930, several of the 100 mines in the area were producing silver. Even today the Hand mine and a few others are spasmodic producers.

Argenta was originally called Montana. Its founders, who chartered the town site on January 6, 1865, described its location as ". . . consisting of three hundred and twenty acres . . . to wit commencing at a certain stake platted on the south bank of Rattlesnake Creek near the mouth of a certain dry gulch or Ravine a short distance below a long pine tree running in a southerly direction one-half mile. Thence Easterly one mile, thence Northerly to Rattlesnake Creek thence up said creek to a point of beginning."[2]

The following year, the first smelter in Montana territory was built at Argenta. It was of German design. Charcoal for the smelter was burned on the upper Rattlesnake Creek; bricks for the furnace came from Saint Louis *via* the Missouri River to Fort Benton, then by ox-team to the smelter site.

Of the state's mining towns, Argenta is probably the emotional favorite of most Montanans. From the smelters of Argenta came the counterparts of "cartwheels," or silver dollars. Joaquin Miller wrote, "The St. Louis smelting furnace ran out the argentiferous galena at Argenta into base bullion, which their cupel furnace reduced to discs of pure silver as large as new moons. As these broad discs of white metal were displayed in the bank windows of Eastern cities, the fame of Golconda and El Dorado paled before the rising glories of Argenta."[3]

The Hand Stamp Mine above Argenta. The district is the second oldest quartz camp in the state

Argenta was never a brawling mining place,[4] for it was an organized company town. Wild, individualistic miners were not attracted to such a setting, nor could they afford to set up large and expensive operations to mine and process the quartz. For a time there were active gold placers as well as silver quartz lodes. During the 1860s, its population was about 1,500. Although there were six saloons, the ratio of saloons to other business establishments was low; for there were three hotels, two grocery stores, one drygoods store, two butcher shops, two blacksmith shops, one bakery, one tailor shop and one dancehall.[5] There was no church, and no schoolhouse. School terms were held with more regularity than in most mining towns. "A term never lasted more than three months as it was difficult to maintain enrollment or to keep teachers for long in an unorganized society. Teachers were paid either by local subscription or by benefit dances held in a home or in a saloon. The usual salary was twenty dollars a month plus room and board that was furnished week about by different families in the town."[6]

1. Bannack was the first.
2. Jean Davis, *Shallow Diggin's*, Caxton Printers, Caldwell, Idaho, 1966, p. 103.
3. Joaquin Miller, *An Illustrated History of the State of Montana*, Lewis Publishing Company, Chicago, 1894, p. 691.
4. Although there is a report of a sheepherder with a gun and a Chinaman with a bloody Bowie-knife who one night made much noise, but caused no damage.
5. Muriel Sibell Wolle, *Montana Pay Dirt*, Sage Books, Denver, 1963, p. 47.
6. Davis, pp. 104-05. What is presumably meant by board furnished "week about" is that each week a different family would host the teachers.

BASIN:

Where the walls came a' tumbling down.

Miners' cabins were the first buildings near, and in, what is now Basin. From the 1860s until Basin City was founded in 1880, mining activity was slow. Most mining required extensive and expensive mills, concentrators, and other equipment; and caught between high smelting charges and low silver prices, many mines in the Boulder area closed before the turn of the century.

Throughout the years, mines have opened, prospered, and closed, sometimes to begin the cycle again. The architecture of Basin reflects these fluctuations. The huge jib mill, which dates back to the 1900s, looms large and ghostly on the edeg of town.

The townsite itself has bulged and shrunk, accommodating nearly 8,000 people during boom times, as few as 220 today. Optimistic plans which never materialized are reflected by a huge smokestack on the edge of town. A smelter was planned and begun, but never completed.

The ravages of time and vandals are everywhere apparent. The Keeley Brothers saloon and restaurant had been closed for years, everything intact, waiting, like most of Basin, for another flurry of mining activity. In 1968 vandals broke the back bar mirror and carted away everything of value. Some Basinites muse at the coincidence that about the time the saloon-restaurant was broken into, an antique dealer was in town looking for articles to buy.

Basin has suffered the ravages of many fires. The fire of 1893 leveled much of the town. In 1893 the Katy mill had been enlarged. Only one successful run of ore had gone through it when it, the hoisting plant, and the shaft were destroyed by fire. The concentrator at the Hope gold mine caught fire in 1896, killing seven miners by suffocation. Today, Basin doesn't even have a firehouse. The owner of a saloon which adjoined the firehouse tore down his building. Since the two structures were connected, when the saloon wall came tumbling down, so did the fire-station wall.

One of many reminders of Basin's heyday

An ore car in Basin Gulch. Within a few feet of the car, an active tramway cuts across the road

Keeley Brothers Saloon and Restaurant in Basin

A monument to empty dreams. No ore was ever processed through this semi-completed smelter at Basin

Despite efforts of the volunteer fire department, Basin suffered from the ravages of several fires. In 1968, when the owner of the saloon which adjoined the fire house, tore down his structure, a wall of the fire house came down with it. Present plans call for rebuilding the fire station in a new location

BEARMOUTH:

A town that barely made it.

Bearmouth is about five miles down the gulch from Beartown. And when Beartown and Garnet died, so did Bearmouth. It had existed only to serve as a trading and transportation center for the towns and camps up Bear Gulch.

The rich ores from the Gulch, Springtown, Top O'Deep, Copper Cliff, Yreka, and Reynolds City had funneled down the trails to Bearmouth, from there to be shipped to smelters in Helena, Butte or Anaconda.

Bearmouth never was large, sporting primarily a stagecoach stop and inn, livery stable, blacksmith shop, and some scattered buildings.

John Lannen[1] operated a small cable-operated ferry across the Clark Fork River. One day the cable snapped while pulling two men and three mules packing 250-gallon barrels of whiskey. Although one man drowned, all three whiskey barrels were recovered. The river also posed seasonal problems for the mailman. In winter he could make his deliveries over the ice cover, but during the other seasons he forded it with mail pouch held high above his head.

Bearmouth was a stopover point for stagecoaches which plied the old Mullan Road between Fort Benton, Montana and Walla Walla, Washington.[2]

Even buildings as solidly constructed as this could not withstand the assaults of the "Beartown Roughs"

Stages plying the rough terrain between Fort Benton, Montana and Walla Walla, Washington, stopped at the remodeled Bearmouth stagecoach stop shown on the right

1. Other reports indicate Chris Lannen owned the ferry and most other businesses in Bearmouth.
2. The stagecoach stop and inn have been moved and remodeled, and are presently occupied.

BEARTOWN:

It needed its "Guardians of Public Morality".

Coloma, Garnet, Beartown, and Bearmouth are interrelated, being on Bear Gulch or its adjoining canyons.

Of the four, only Beartown has disappeared.

One wag said the history of Beartown reads like a wild collaboration between Edgar Allan Poe, Jules Verne, and George Orwell, as told by someone on a bad LSD trip.

That's not quite accurate.

Any historical assessment of Beartown must include reporting of a number of incidents which might be difficult for modern man to believe. It's even more difficult to comprehend these shenanigans and carryings-on after visiting vanished Beartown.

Gold was discovered here in 1865. Today, hand-lettered signs, not exactly in impeccable American-ese, explain something of the history of this town which became the trading center for about 5,000 miners.

Remains of a dug-out which once served as a powder storage vault can be detected. The structure later served as a jail. Accounts about existence in this home of the "Beartown Roughs" clearly indicate more than one place of incarceration might have been desirable, if not mandatory. Prisoners were often taken to nearby Deer Lodge, to what has been described as the most "unretentive" jail in the nation, as it never held a prisoner long enough to bring him to justice.[1]

Here are highlights from a few of the newspaper âccounts and word-of-mouth tales about Beartown, Montana.

Dr. Armistead "Mit" Mitchell of Deer Lodge sporadically rode over to Beartown just for a few fingers of redeye or to offer his professional services.

The doctor's professional reputation was good while sober and superior when drunk.

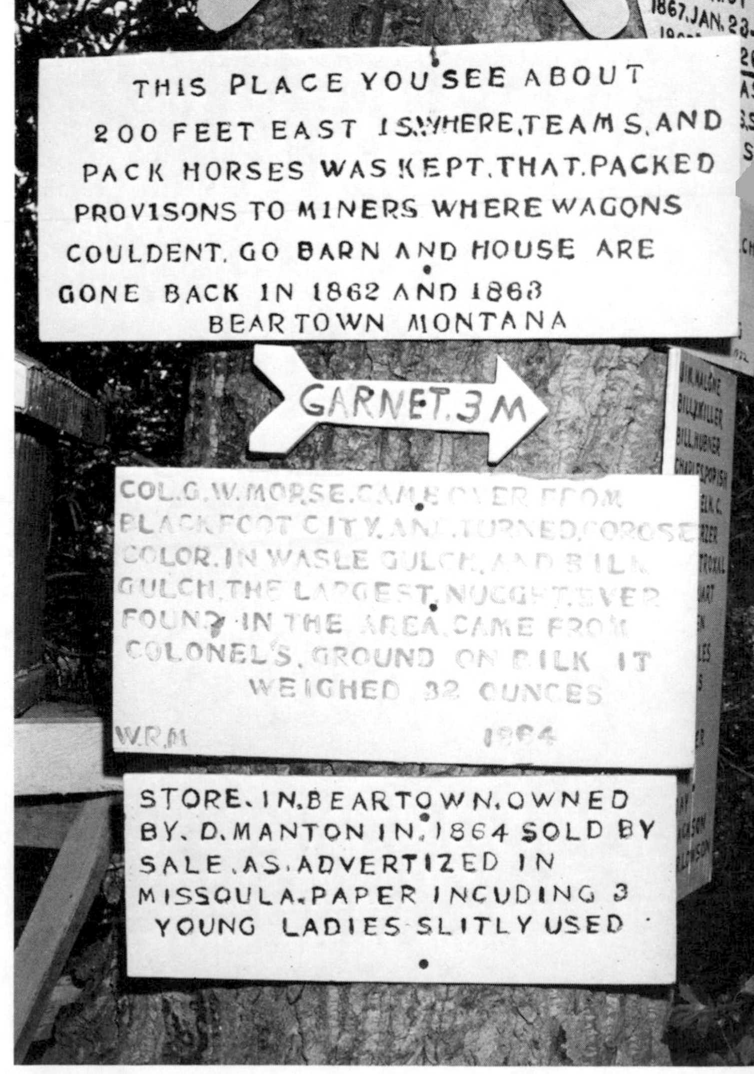

Signs recently posted at Beartown tell something of the history of the home of the "Beartown Roughs"

Muriel Sibell Wolle in *The Bonanza Trail* describes "Mit's" ministering to one of Beartown's citizens:

> One morning he arrived at Abascal's store to perform an operation on Shorty, who had the misfortune, while dead drunk, to stumble into his own fireplace and lie with his arm in the embers all night until it was burned to a crisp. As soon as "Mit" had sawed off the arm and bound up the stump in a soiled rag, Shorty, still fortified against pain by whisky, ran to the door and called in his friends for a round of drinks. While the boys crowded around the patient, "Mit" collected the scraps of flesh and bone and put them in a gunny sack to take home, with some fuzzy idea of using them in an experiment he was conducting. The board and two whisky barrels that had served as the operating table were put away, and Shorty, the doctor, and two or three cronies sat down to an all day game of poker. That evening a dance was held at Pelletier's [saloon] and everyone went. It was daylight when it broke up, and the doctor lurched to his horse, carrying the sack of charred bones. Somewhere along the trail home he lost the arm.[2]

Mrs. Wolle also describes the antics of Old Greenwood:

> [He] . . . worked a claim several miles down the gulch and had no partner except the one he invented, with whom he carried on constant abusive arguments. He would shovel gravel at the bottom of his shaft, and when he was ready to hoist the bucket, he would yell up to his "partner." After waiting awhile, he would climb to the surface and cuss out his nonexisent helper before proceeding to haul up the dirt himself.[3]

There was this account of a not-usually-rough "Beartown Rough", in the *Missoula and Cedar Creek Pioneer*, May 25, 1871:

> Considerable excitement was created in the pastoral hamlet of Beartown a few evenings since by the surreptitious introduction into camp, by some outside barbarian, of a singular fluid known as "benzine botheration." One of the "Fathers of Israel" there resident incautiously partook of the dangerous compound, which produced an effect upon his usually placid brain of the most unexpected character. He proceeded to demolish the windows and doors of a *maison d' joie* at the upper end of town, and emptied a double barreled shotgun among the inmates. The citizens threw themselves into a hollow square for the purpose of restraining these unlawful proceedings, when the "little discussion" with clubs and six-shooters became general. Shortly after the smoke of battle had cleared away, the Guardians of Public Morality held a special meeting to take steps for the enlargement of the village graveyard.[4]

The Guardians of Public Morality were Beartown's version of vigilantes.

Although the "village graveyard" spoken of did exist (seven were buried there), most of Beartown's dead were buried in the cemetery at Deer Lodge. It seems there weren't proper plots for a good "marble orchard" at Beartown. The gulch was narrow, but there was a slope above the creek which was terraced with stones, so heavy rains and mudslides wouldn't wash bodies down the hill.

Jean Davis, in *Shallow Diggin's*, gives this account of the funeral of a member of Beartown's ethnic majority in the more adequate Deer Lodge interment grounds:

> It was in Bear Gulch in the winter of '70. At that time there were no wagon roads, only trails, but Bear Town was a prosperous mining camp, cutting straight across as we did, in the neighborhood of 35 miles from Deer Lodge. We were drifting and hoisting pay dirt to wash in the spring; and the diggin's were deep.
>
> Mike Flynn—we called him Micky Finn—lived the third claim below us and in the winter he got sick. We visited him several times and finally Micky died.
>
> Micky was a good Christian and his partner had promised him that he would bury him in consecrated ground. We miners agreed upon the advice of Joaquin Abascal, to get our horses and bury Micky in Deer Lodge in the consecrated burying ground.
>
> We started out one morning from Micky's cabin. We had the corpse rolled up in a blanket and thrown over an Arapahoe pack saddle. One of the boys led the horse that was carrying it behind his own. There was quite a string of us.
>
> Near the mouth of Bear Creek we found a man who had his rip-saw set up in the woods. Some of us stayed there to saw enough lumber to make a coffin for poor Micky, while some of us went into the Bitter Root to Baron O'Keefe to borrow an old democrat wagon and harness. We had quite a time breaking the cayuses into harness, which wasn't very strong. It was made of Shaganapy, which is a kind of Indian leather.
>
> Well, we put the corpse in the coffin and placed it in the wagon in the back. Next morning when we got ready to pull out for Deer Lodge we had another circus gettin' the horses started, but after breakfast the procession started, those on horseback going ahead. It was quite a procession. We traveled until we got to Gold Creek. At Pioneer bar there was some ground sluice and we found there was a saloon.
>
> As it was late in the afternoon some of the boys went in and had a drink. And pretty soon

they went in and had another drink. Then we concluded that as poor Micky had never had a wake we would bring him in and hold a real Irish wake. We got some candles and brought the coffin in and set it on two beer kegs. We took off the lid and lighted the candles and there was poor Micky a layin' in there. We had some real good singin' and drinkin' all night. The boys all got pretty tired and so we made our beds on the floor around the coffin.

In the morning as we had to go on, we had a miner make us some coffee and we started out on our journey toward Deer Lodge. The boys were pretty well worn out so that in the afternoon the storekeeper said to me and Jim to ride on ahead and see the priest and tell him we was comin' and to dig the grave for Micky. So the two of us spurred up our horses and got to Deer Lodge and saw the father and told him to show us the place to dig the grave. He was very kind to us and gave us some supper. Then we dug the grave and it was pretty dark. It took us a while to finish and when we were done the father came out with his cassock and his book and told us that the work was done in a good workmanlike manner.

As we were waiting for the procession we finally saw it coming down the valley. All of us stood in respectful position ready for the burial of poor Micky. And finally as the wagon pulled up, Lord and behold the corpse was gone. I tell you we sure felt badly. The two drivers said that comin' down the hill the wagon had run up on the horses' hind quarters and of course they reared around acting as though they wanted to shake hands with the driver. We all felt pretty bad and were ashamed of ourselves. The father said for us to go to Deer Lodge for the night and in the morning some of us could look up the corpse and bury it.

We all went to Deer Lodge and had a meeting in Pete Valiton's brewery. The next morning Jim and I and two more started out from Deer Lodge in the wagon. At the top of the hill we found the place where the horses had acted up and after a long search we finally found the coffin down in the creek bed where it rolled. And there was poor Micky standin' on his head. We had an awful time gettin' the water out of the coffin, but we brought the body up reverently to Deer Lodge and buried it with proper ceremonies.[5]

Beartown had the usual number of business establishments including a wash house, a drugstore, a slaughterhouse, a brewery, a general store, a hotel, and Pelletier's saloon—one of the few two-story structures.

Pelletier's was the heart of community activity, for here was the home of Chicago Joe's dance hall girls.

The pay was pretty good, but the work was hard.

Although the ladies normally "rented" their talents, the Guardians of Public Morality decided some might go up for sale on the auction block. Henry Lamb and Company, Auctioneers, advertised in the *Missoula and Cedar Creek Pioneer* on April 27, 1871, that:

> In accordance with instructions received from the Guardians of Public Morality of the City of Beartown, M.T., we will dispose of by public vendue, on the 1st day of May, 1871, at 2 o'clock p.m., opposite the store of D. Manton, in said city, to the highest bidder for cash, three charming young ladies, whose morals have been slightly damaged by sea-water in transit from New York. The articles are almost as good as new, and will be sold at a sacrifice to close consignments.
>
> Henry Lamb & Co., *Auctioneers*

The "outside world" heard nothing more of the proposed auction until May 11th, when the same publication carried a notice from a member of the Beartown vigilance committee stating:

> The sale of the three *nymphs du pave*, advertised to come off here on the 1st inst., has been postponed on account of the scarcity of purchasers.
>
> A GUARDIAN OF BEARTOWN MORALITY

This town, one-time runner-up for state capital, is a good town for the armchair ghost towner; for what it lacks in physical remains, it more than makes up for in a colorful, rich history.

However, many visitors to Beartown go there for an exciting, but so far fruitless mission—to try to find the five-pound baking powder tins of gold a Chinaman reportedly hid near there.

1. Vardis Fisher, *Gold Rushes and Mining Camps of the Early American West*, Caxton Printers Ltd., Caldwell, Idaho, 1968, p. 303.
2. Muriel Sibell Wolle, *The Bonanza Trail*, Indiana University Press, Bloomington, 1953, p. 209.
3. *Ibid.*, p. 210.
4. *Missoula and Cedar Creek Pioneer*, Missoula, Montana, May 25, 1871.
5. Davis, *Shallow Diggin's*, 141-142. Originally in *Silver State Post* (Deer Lodge), March 19, 1942.

Castle, about 1891—Courtesy, Montana Historical Society

Minnie's "Sporting House" in Castle

The boarding house at Castle

CASTLE: And the return, because of brandy, of a "dead man".

The ghost town of Castletown was named after the castle-like rocks adorning nearby Castle Mountain, near White Sulphur Springs.

Outcroppings were discovered in the area as early as 1882, but little mining was done until 1884 and 1885. At one time Castle was considered one of the richest mining camps in the state. Copper king Marcus Daly invested heavily in mines in the area, as did many other capitalists. As Castle mushroomed, it sported a $5,000 schoolhouse, eighty dwellings, a jail, fourteen saloons and seven brothels.

Although three stage lines provided daily service to four other area towns, Castle needed a railroad to haul its mail, ore, mining machinery, coke, and people. Promoter par excellence Richard A. Harlow set out to give the people what they wanted. In polite social circles Harlow was known as a "jawboner"—one who was long on talk and short on funds. Somehow he managed to get the sixty-mile railroad built at a cost of nearly $3,000,000. The project took ten years. In 1898, a spring flood washed out part of the roadbed, which had to be rebuilt. Finally, in 1903, Harlow had completed his railroad, perhaps called "The Jawbone" in honor of its builder. Another theory is that the railroad was so-named because the route it traversed roughly corresponded to the shape of the jawbone of an animal. The Northern Pacific expressed interest in the road, and when it asked Harlow what towns were on the line, he made up names for non-existent communities. He later confided, ". . . strangely a number are on the map today. Two young ladies (Fan and Lulu) were visiting at my house. On the timetable as a result you will find Fanalulu just below Ringling."[1]

Bill Gay and his sidekick brother-in-law Gross (no known first name) caused some excitement in Castle in 1890. Gay had discovered a coal lead. Later he discovered Benson, the editor of the newspaper, in the mine shaft. Though claim jumping was common in Castle, and there was a vigilante committee, Gay took matters into his own hands by throwing the windlass rope down the shaft. Benson, left with no means of exit, set up a furor which attracted attention. A lawsuit resulted. Fifty witnesses were summoned to testify at the trial. The witnesses for both sides stopped at a stage station near Townsend on the way to Helena for the trial. It appears the witnesses couldn't calmly discuss both sides of the issue. When they arrived in Helena, there were a number of bloody knuckles and black eyes.

Apparently Mr. Benson was the winner of the trial, for when it was over Gay and Gross set the torch to Benson's print shop and, while they were at it, set fire to several other structures in town. After some other side incidents, a posse tried to hunt them down. They weren't found. Later, Gay was picked up in Needles, California, and extradited to Montana. Two deputies attempted to apprehend Gross in Saint Louis, Missouri. He escaped and was not heard of again.

By the early 1890s, Castle was virtually deserted. By 1927 most of the abandoned claims were sold for taxes by Meagher County. By 1936 only two people lived in Castle—75-year-old "Mayor" Joseph Hooker Kidd and 70-year-old constable Joseph Martino. Kidd's death was the next-to-last chapter in the death of Castle.

It was a bitter winter, with snow drifts up to forty feet. Provisions were almost gone, so Kidd hitched up his team and cutter[2] and headed for Lennep, seven miles away.

The first day Kidd made only three miles, staying the night at a sheep camp. He finally made it to Lennep, got the mail and supplies and headed back. He spent the night at a ranch, and the next day managed to get within a mile of Castle before his team gave out. He walked the rest of the way, arriving at 9:00 P.M. After a hot cup of coffee at Martino's cabin, Kidd headed for his home, 500 yards away. En route he collapsed and died. Martino was too weak to carry the body, so he covered it with a blanket. Martino made the three-mile trip, on skis, to the sheep camp. Three days later the sheriff and coroner from White Sulphur Springs skied into Castle, placed Kidd's body on a toboggan, and left Joseph Martino as the sole resident.

Years after Castle was deserted, some mining engineers were picking through rubbish at the rear of one of the saloons. They uncovered a rich strike:

> The discovery consisted of 10 gallons of Three Star Hennessey brandy in a barrel, where it had reposed since the closing of the saloon some time shortly after 1893. It is claimed that one of the discovery party maintained it should be used for strictly medicinal purposes. The others, however, stood unanimously for a division of the resources.
>
> After a long and voluble meeting it was decided to divvy up with every man in camp, and that Whispering Johnson could keep his for medicinal or social purposes as he saw fit. . . .
>
> The camp usually boasts a dozen men, counting in the entire population of Castle mountains. However, 20 gathered for the division, one man coming in from the hills, a fellow who hadn't been seen for years and reported lost in the blizzard of 1911. The division resulted in an equal share of one-half gallon each, with a few shots left over, which were not left for long.
>
> The following resolutions were adopted by the meeting:
>
> Whereas, the world has forgotten Castle for a long time, and
>
> Whereas, the unfounded rumor has been circulated that no more pay streaks can ever again be uncovered in the old camp, therefore, be it
>
> Resolved, that Saturday night shall be declared a holiday, to celebrate the coming of prosperity to Castle, to again use the old tables and paraphernalia found in the old building, to consult again the spots on divers pasteboard, and in other ways and means, duly have a party.
>
> They did.[3]

(Brandy was not generally considered a favorite alcoholic beverage on the mining frontier. Whiskey was first choice. On those rare occasions when the whiskey ran out, the ingenious bartenders would brew up some "tanglefoot," made by mixing boiled mountain sage, two plugs of tobacco, and one box of cayenne pepper with one gallon of water. A shot of "tanglefoot" commonly went for two bits.)[4]

At this writing, active mining is going on in the vicinity of Castle Town. Some mining operations are being undertaken in the Castle Canyon, and the Cumberland mine above the town site is in operation.

One interesting sight in contemporary Castle is a house with hand-cut shingles.

1. H. G. Stearns, "Know Montana: The Jawbone Railroad," *Dillon Daily Tribune*, (*See also* Harold J. Stearns *A History of the Upper Musselshell Valley to 1920*, thesis, University of Montana. 1966.)
2. A small, light sleigh, usually single-seated and pulled by one horse.
3. *Scobey Sentinel*, October 8, 1926.
4. William S. Greever, *The Bonanza West*, University of Oklahoma Press, 1963, p. 231.

Once this now rotting trunk probably held precious family treasures—Courtesy, Carl Hansen

COLOMA:

Mystery camp of the Garnet Range.

An old store at Coloma—Courtesy, Carl Hansen

Coloma is a couple of miles above Garnet at the end of a pocked and rutted trail, speckled with boulders.

Mines remain near the site, and a few, including some with possibly profitable deposits, are still occasionally worked during the summer.

Many of the buildings of Coloma are not as old as those of Garnet, and newspapers and magazines of the 1920s and 1930s are strewn on many cabin floors. These materials, plus pages from mail order catalogs, were commonly used to paper the cabin walls for insulation.

Mine shafts, rusting ventilation systems, and pumping machines abound, and the town holds the remains of narrow-gauge railroad tracks which were used in hauling out the ores. Sounds of logging trucks and present-day mining operations break the silence most visitors expect of a ghost town.

Coloma's early history is shrouded in mystery. U.S. geological survey teams, in United States Geological Survey *Bulletin* 660 (p. 195), described abortive attempts to glean information about Coloma in 1917:

"During 1896 and the next few years, while the Mammoth and Comet mines were in operation, it was lively. In 1916 there was some activity—mills were installed . . . but from all that could be learned neither mine yielded a profit. . . . Although rich in places, the veins are small, and the work seems to have been planned on a scale out of proportion to them."

The *Bulletin* indicated that no mining records were seen, but estimated that about $200,000 in gold ore taken from the Mammonth mine. Most of the ore, it reported, was milled, and all but a little of the gold was lost in tailings. The report continued (p. 196), "None of the old workings were accessible at the time of the visit, and information concerning the ore bodies is rather meager."

Even today, it is most difficult to find facts about this obscure mining town. The long-time postmistress of nearby Greenough maintains ,"There are so many new logging roads in the area, I couldn't begin to tell you where the town is." Area residents who know about the town refuse to answer questions about it.

Perhaps mining operations at Coloma were monumental failures which no one wishes to admit. Perhaps Coloma is one of those areas where the possibility of wealthy discoveries is still great enough to silence those who might tell of its past, present and possible future.

The remains of what was probably the blacksmith's shop at Coloma—Courtesy, Carl Hansen

NOTICE NOTICE NOTICE NOTICE

THIS IS PRIVATE PROPERTY AND TO ENTER OR TO ATTEMPT TO ENTER ANY OF THESE BUILDINGS IS TO TRESPASS. THESE BUILDINGS ARE LOCKED AND BOARDED UP FOR A REASON AND THAT IS TO KEEP PEOPLE OUT!!

THIS PROPERTY IS BEING WATCHED BY A NUMBER OF PERSONS IN THIS AREA—SO HEED THIS WARNING!!!!

JUST CONSIDER THAT YOUR PROPERTY IS OF SOME VALUE TO YOU THEN THIS PROPERTY IS OF VALUE TO THESE OWNERS—AND THEY ARE PAYING TAXES ON IT!!!!

JUST LOOK AT SOME OF THE BUILDINGS IN THIS MINING CAMP AND HOW THEY HAVE GONE TO RUIN BECAUSE INCONSIDERATE PEOPLE HAVE KICKED THE DOORS DOWN AND BROKEN THE WINDOWS OUT. THESE BUILDINGS WERE AT ONE TIME GOOD SHELTERS AND ESPECIALLY DURING THE WINTER MONTHS WHEN IT IS 40 AND 50 DEGREES BELOW ZERO AND A PERSON MAY BE STRANDED HERE. SO TREAT THIS PROPERTY LIKE YOU WOULD LIKE TO HAVE SOMEONE TREAT YOURS!!!

FOR THE OWNERS

(SIGNED) JOHN GIULIO, JR.
COMET AND HIGHMORE GULCH PROTECTIVE ASSOCIATION.

COMET:

So heed this warning!

Despite warning signs and locked doors, Comet is being vandalized

So reads the warning to those who come to disturb the repose of Comet, Montana.

Comet lies near Basin in what is known as the Cataract Mining District. Records of the first mining activity in the area are hazy. The father and uncle of John Giulio, Jr., present spokesman for the Basin Montana Tunnel Company (formerly owned by the

The boarding house at Comet

Montana Consolidated Copper Company), maintain the first operations began about 1875.

Almost all areas in the townsite are on patented land, except for plats off the ore vein system.

The present-day town consists of about two dozen buildings in various states of disrepair: the boarding house; mill superintendent's home, intact with swing on porch; hotel; a schoolhouse; livery stable; several houses; and the giant mill of the Basin Montana Tunnel Company. Water for the mill was supplied by the nearby creek, while water for the town was brought in by flume from a spring about two miles away and stored in a still-standing water tower.

The town reportedly sported twenty-two saloons at one time. As Rosie's boardinghouse, miners who commonly received $3.90 per shift could find room and board for 75 cents a day, leaving some left over for frolicking with the "soiled doves" in nearby parlor houses[1] and a few shots of "pop-skull."[2]

Unofficial estimates put the number of pupils attending the Comet school in 1930 at twenty, with a total mill-mine employment figure of 300.

For several years publications of the U.S. Geological Survey list the Comet mine as the largest producer in the mining district, yielding primarily underground lead-zinc ores and lead.

Typical company reports in the 1930s were:

John Giulio, Jr., a third-generation owner of property in Comet, decries recent vandalism. He says, "They tore apart my grandparents' house, even removing the piano. Every door and every window in the town is gone. When doors and windows are broken, it gives buildings a five-year life. It weakens the structures, the wind blows through, the snow

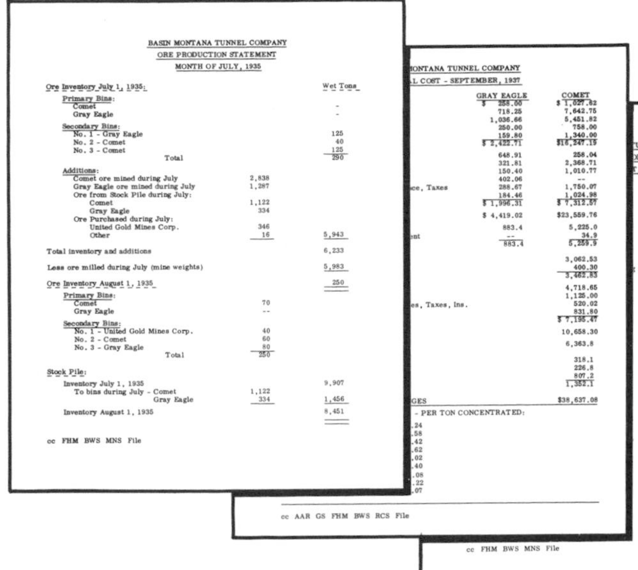

BASIN MONTANA TUNNEL COMPANY
ORE PRODUCTION STATEMENT
MONTH OF JULY, 1935

		Wet Tons
Ore Inventory July 1, 1935:		
Primary Bins:		
Comet		-
Gray Eagle		-
Secondary Bins:		
No. 1 - Gray Eagle		125
No. 2 - Comet		40
No. 3 - Comet		125
Total		290
Additions:		
Comet ore mined during July	2,838	
Gray Eagle ore mined during July	1,287	
Ore from Stock Pile during July:		
Comet	1,122	
Gray Eagle	334	
Ore Purchased during July:		
United Gold Mines Corp.	346	
Other	16	5,943
Total inventory and additions		6,233
Less ore milled during July (mine weights)		5,983
Ore Inventory August 1, 1935		250
Primary Bins:		
Comet	70	
Gray Eagle	--	
Secondary Bins:		
No. 1 - United Gold Mines Corp.	40	
No. 2 - Comet	60	
No. 3 - Gray Eagle	80	
Total	250	
Stock Pile:		
Inventory July 1, 1935		9,907
To bins during July - Comet	1,122	
Gray Eagle	334	1,456
Inventory August 1, 1935		8,451

cc FHM BWS MNS File

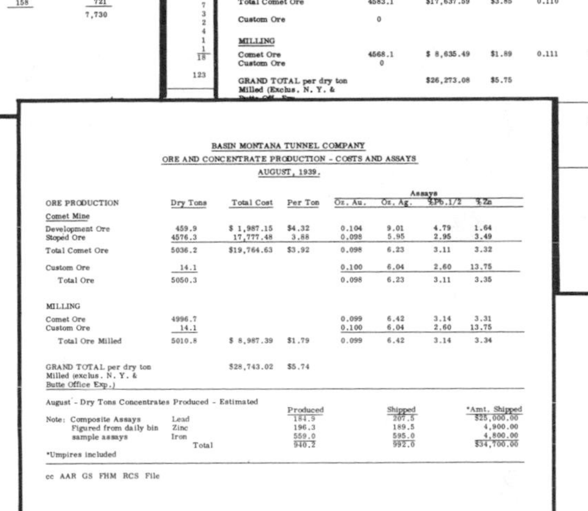

BASIN MONTANA TUNNEL COMPANY
ORE AND CONCENTRATE PRODUCTION - COSTS AND ASSAYS
AUGUST, 1939.

ORE PRODUCTION	Dry Tons	Total Cost	Per Ton	Assays Oz. Au.	Oz. Ag.	%Pb.1/2	%Zn
Comet Mine							
Development Ore	459.9	$ 1,987.15	$4.32	0.104	9.01	4.79	1.64
Stoped Ore	4576.3	17,777.48	3.88	0.098	5.95	2.95	3.49
Total Comet Ore	5036.2	$19,764.63	$3.92	0.098	6.23	3.11	3.32
Custom Ore	14.1			0.100	6.04	2.60	13.75
Total Ore	5050.3			0.098	6.23	3.11	3.35
MILLING							
Comet Ore	4996.7			0.099	6.42	3.14	3.31
Custom Ore	14.1			0.100	6.04	2.60	13.75
Total Ore Milled	5010.8	$ 8,987.39	$1.79	0.099	6.42	3.14	3.34
GRAND TOTAL per dry ton Milled (exclus. N. Y. & Butte Office Exp.)		$28,743.02	$5.74				

August - Dry Tons Concentrates Produced - Estimated

Note: Composite Assays Figured from daily bin sample assays		Produced	Shipped	*Amt. Shipped
	Lead	184.9	207.5	$25,000.00
	Zinc	196.3	189.5	4,900.00
	Iron	559.0	595.0	4,800.00
	Total	940.2	992.0	$34,700.00

*Umpires included

cc AAR GS FHM RCS File

Complete reports are shown on pages 174-177

Rosie's "fun house"

A view of the Comet mill from the veranda of the mine superintendent's home

A gate nestled beneath a tramway near Comet

comes in, the elements take over. Don't write about Comet. Since a *Great Falls* [Montana] *Tribune* article came out in the summer of 1970, vandals did more damage in three weeks than had been done in many years. Most of Comet's old-timers are dead and gone; but what I've heard, I've tried to record. But I don't want anyone else to hear about it. If they did, the town would be completely ruined."[3]

When asked how to keep away people bent on ransacking the town, Giulio replied, "I have a 30.30 rifle."

Giulio further stated that mostly people from area towns cause the depredation, and "even if you stood guard twenty hours a day, during the other four hours, they'd come and ruin the place."

The giant Comet mine mill still stands, not completely ruined, on a mountainside above the town. Wind whistles through the gaunt buildings, sagebrush gives off its pungent odors, stable doors swing, a flag pole still stands—sans flag; cattle roam the townsite—and Comet, perhaps Montana's finest "unpreserved" ghost town, squats, soon to succumb to the ravages of climate and people. It can only be hoped that when Comet is dead and gone, John Giulio, Jr. will release the background information he has accumulated on this—one of Montana's four or five best ghost towns. But perhaps there are some good reasons why he shouldn't release the information.

Blueprints and financial reports of the Basin Montana Tunnel Company litter this company house in Comet

A huge settling pond is located across the road from this structure

When the stairs became unsafe, this ladder provided access . . . now the ladder is unsafe

1. Giulio maintains there was never a "fun house" in Comet; others disagree. Several reports indicate Rosie ran a whorehouse.
2. Booze.
3. Personal interview, October 5, 1970.

ELKHORN:

Where the Cross of Gold oration was given.

Note the ornate front of Fraternity Hall (right)

South of Helena is a classic, scantily-inhabited ghost town—Elkhorn.

From the false-fronted balconied Fraternity Brothers Hall to the bullet marks on cabins, to the emporium, to broken window glass, to creaking doors, to the hotels, to the Elkhorn and Midnight Bell Queen and Golden Curry mines, to the cemetery perched high above the fairly well-preserved town, down to the sagebrush on the streets, Elkhorn measures up to preconceptions most visitors have of what a ghost town is supposed to look like. And to top it off, scenes from the television documentary "The Real West," narrated by Gary Cooper, were filmed at Elkhorn.

Silver, gold, and lead poured from the mines: $14,000,000 in silver alone.

Everything that mining normally brings it brought to Elkhorn: disease, homicide, mining and woodcutting accidents, supply problems, fires, brutal hours of work, hurdy gurdies and saloons, prostitution, gambling. All timber is second-growth, evidence of the work of the 500 wood cutters out to get the cordwood needed to supply the needs of the mill and homes in Elkhorn. They used about 1,500 head of horses to haul that precious wood to the mill and about seventy-five structures which were originally a part of the town.

A fascination for some visitors to Elkhorn is a huge wagon which slowly decomposes on the edge of town. The wagon was especially constructed to transport a transformer, that weighed thirty tons, from the railhead to the mill. Twelve head of horses pulled the wagon, twelve head pushed. At the mill, even today, can be found cyanide tanks.

One of Elkhorn's original 14 saloons is pictured on the left, next to the Fraternity Hall

A view of nearly half of the extensive Elkhorn ghost town

Dynamite crates "make do" for finished walls on a cabin at Dagotown

It was here that orator William Jennings Bryan delivered his famous "Cross of Gold" speech.

Signs indicate where candy stores and saloons or other business establishments once stood. A picnic ground is at the edge of town, and the site is relatively easy to get to by car. One sign points to a still-standing "dog house," complete with bed behind a regular house where the man of the house presumably could retreat to avoid his wife's scolding.

The cemetery is well-maintained. It had been preserved by a group from the Boulder River school during the 1960s. Stone and wooden markers spanning a century are there. Markers at head and foot are common, as are metal and wooden paling fences surrounding grave sites. The markers tell of a diphtheria epidemic[1] which claimed the lives of many infants and children primarily during the summer of 1889.

Concentrates from the Elkhorn mill being loaded for shipment about 1908—Courtesy, Fred Bell, Sr.

Near Elkhorn[2] were the settlements of Dagotown and Sourdough. A half dozen structures remain at Dagotown, but all traces of Sourdough have disappeared.

A tiny general store and curio shop is the only operating business in town. In 1972 the Elkhorn mine, which had been shut down in 1912, was being pumped of water down to the 500-foot level in anticipation of reactivating the mine; but chances appear slim that the town of Elkhorn will be reborn.

In 1972 the Fraternity Brothers Hall and adjacent structure were purchased by the Western Montana Ghost Town Preservation Society. The society is intent upon stabilizing the two structures. The Fraternity Brothers Hall is considered to be one of the most historically significant western American structures still standing.

On Memorial Days, Fred Bell, Sr., who was born in Elkhorn in 1898—son of a blacksmith—brings his historic pictures and other memorabilia of the town and holds what he terms a "bullshow," to pass on to tourists tidbits of history of Elkhorn.

Among Mr. Bell's statistics: only two funerals and one murder occurred in the Fraternity Brothers Hall, headquarters for chapters of half a dozen organizations. He also tells of a "teetotalling" lodge chapter housed in a structure sandwiched between two saloons.

And so, annually, a hearty voice from Elkhorn's past reverberates through the cadaverous structures of Elkhorn, Montana. As Mr. Bell feels, the "bullshow must go on." But the final curtain must soon fall, and a living bit of a rich history will soon be stilled, never to be heard again.

In the well-kept Elkhorn cemetery can be found much western history. Lambs atop children's markers, reflect on a diphtheria epidemic which claimed many lives. It is reported that a mother and five children died of the disease over a period of days

Entrance to the Buliver Mine in 1915. Fred Bell and Warren DeCamp owned the mine, one of several in the Elkhorn District—Courtesy, Fred Bell, Sr.

One tale has it that famed orator, William Jennings Bryan stayed, here, at the Grand Hotel during his visit to Elkhorn to deliver the "Cross of Gold" speech

Testimony to the fact that the ashes have long been cold at Dagotown

Prospector, Sam Perrin of Elkhorn —Courtesy, Montana Historical Society

Elkhorn about 1900
—Courtesy, Fred Bell, Sr.

1. An article in the *Helena Independent Record* of February 27, 1966, says the epidemic was of "malignant scarlet fever," but this seems unlikely.
2. The *Montana Standard*, September 26, 1954, reports Elkhorn was so named because of the large elk herds in the area.

GARNET:

Named after a semi precious stone: a semi precious ghost town.

Garnet (the town and the entire mountain range near it were named for the brown garnet rock found there, used as an abrasive and a semi-precious stone) is one of the more impressive Montana ghost towns.

Situated near the Blackfoot and Clark Fork Rivers east of Missoula, this once-bustling town has a history spanning almost a century.[1]

Like most mining towns, it's in the high country, and the weight of countless tons of winter snows has tumbled many of the buildings. Fire hit Garnet twice and often structures burned were not rebuilt.

During its heyday, Garnet boasted the Garnet Hotel, D. A. McDonald, Prop., with "sample and card rooms in connection." Insurance agent John H. Cole, at the News Office, was advertising weekly in *The Garnet Mining News* his bonds, leases and deeds, or other legal papers. E. C. Lewis, proprietor of the Mascot Saloon was proclaiming, "Just Opened, With Everything New, Clean and Bright," while Connors and Harwood's Saloon claimed it had the best wines, liquors, and cigars, as did the Kelly and Frazer Saloon. The Resort, "As kept by Hugh Leonard, remains as it has always been, the cleanest and best kept . . . SALOON IN TOWN!" Good eight-year-old McBrayer on tap, and the choicest brands of cigars were located at Hugh Leonard's place in West Garnet.

The ads in the *Garnet Mining News* of February 22, 1900, told of Mrs. Lydia E. Pinkham's Vegetable Compound; Vin Mariani, the ideal French tonic for body and brain; claimed children need "something to put their blood in proper condition for spring's changeable weather," and could get it through

Cabin at Copper Cliff—Courtesy, Carl Hansen

This flower-shaped design caused by resin on the end of a log on a cabin at Copper Cliff is pretty, but also shows that the builder didn't let his logs dry out properly. But time was often a luxury the argonauts didn't have—Courtesy, Carl Hansen

"Moore's Revealed Remedy." "Five Drops" was claimed to be "The Pleasantest, Most Powerful and Effective Never-failing Remedy for Rheumatism, Sciatica, Neuralgia, LaGrippe and Catarrh"; and that "He Liveth Long That Liveth Well," with Hood's Sarsaparilla, good especially against the itching and burning of "scrofulous humor."

But there was progress. The weekly newspaper reported the city council of Butte had introduced a bill to prohibit expectoration on the sidewalks, such action leading to a fine ranging from $1 to $100. Whether Garnet had such a law is not known.

The front page of the *Garnet Mining News* was full of roseate reports under the head "Mines and Mining":

"Sam. Ritchey came to Bearmouth Tuesday and went on to Missoula the following day to meet some parties who are contemplating making a deal on some of his Garnet properties.

"Wm. Reeley who is interested in the Copper Cliff mines went to Missoula Wednesday expecting to make a deal on that justly celebrated property.

"At the Shamrock a cross-cut will be run to the vein from the shaft which is under the vein, in a few days. In the meantime stoping continues in the upper levels. The vein will probably be encountered in about five feet.

"Sinking at the Forest is progressing rapidly and the vein continues to hold its own as to width and value. The hoist and pump which has just been put on is doing good work.

"The leasers on the Lead King are still in good ore and doing well.

"The property belonging to Joe. Saville, Wm. Ross and Mrs. Ross is looking better and better as the vein is followed. It looks now as if it would become one [of] Garnet's leading producers.

"The Montana and Denver Reduction Co.'s mill is running again after the cold snap and is said to be doing good work and giving satisfactory results."

The *News* was claiming, "Now is the time for owners of prospects in and around Garnet to make deals and have their property explored. There is plenty of money in the country for this purpose."

Also on the front page was: "The Dancy is temporarily closed down but the property is as good as ever and it will not be long before more men will probably be employed there than ever before."

The seeds of Garnet's demise were also visible on the front page. The same John H. Cole (two times in the ad referred to as JNO H. Cole) who advertised his agency on page four also had two interesting "For Sale" items on February 22, 1900. One ad reads, "For Sale—One first class, well· fitted saloon and fixtures with snbstantial [*sic*] two story building in the best business part of Garnet. This is really a great bargain. Must be sold in 30 days for cash. Call on or address John H. Cole, Garnet, Mont." The other ad indicated there was a six-stamp quartz mill for sale with a "30 horse power boiler, Blake crusher and plates and everything complete. Been run just six hours since leaving the factory and is now in first class condition. Can be purchased at a bargain."

Today, a few business establishments—Kelley's Bar, Dahl's Saloon, a combination barber shop and drugstore, the F. A. Davey store, a livery stable, the three-story Wells Hotel[2]—and about two dozen cabins remain.

The door of the stable swings, hinges crying for oil. In the hotel hang remnants of red wallpaper ordered from a mail order house in Chicago, Kansas City, or Saint Louis. Similar wallpaper has been found in homes in Bodie, California, 1,000 miles away.

There was lode gold at Garnet and hard rock mining.

There were about fifty mines in the area—including the famous Nancy Hanks, which produced $960,000 in rich ore during its peak year of 1896. The total take probably was about $10,000,000. Many millions in gold were taken from the Garnet area from 1862 to 1916 from profitable mines like the Dewey. The Nancy Hanks continued to operate spasmodically until 1954.

The Nancy Hanks was the richest. One of the two partners who owned the mine liked his booze.

A bird house and weather vane once perched atop this barn at Cable. In 1970 or 1971 they disappeared —Courtesy, Ken Ring

Copper Cliff, near Garnet, was discovered in 1890 by W. P. Shipler. Never classified as a successful mining camp, only a few hundred dollars in copper, silver and gold were taken from this remote Montana mining camp—Courtesy, Carl Hansen

After guzzling a final pint, he sold out to his partner for a reported $50 and moved down the gulch to Beartown, where he spent his last days in frustration. After seeing one of many rich loads of ore from the mine that had been his passing down the trail to the smelters, he hanged himself. (A former resident of Garnet maintains the despondent man didn't hang himself, but rather took a heavy hammer and a mining pick, and drove the heavy metal instrument into the side of his head, causing his death.)[3]

One of the town's most successful entrepreneurs was F. A .Davey, owner of the Garnet General Store, the Wells Hotel, the Garnet Stage Line and the Garnet Freight Line.

Frank Davey was apparently disliked by the children, and they sometimes played tricks on the man. Occasionally they would order candy from him and pay him in rocks. One day, in retaliation for what the children thought was unfair treatment, they hanged him in effigy from the hotel flagpole.

Davey reportedly kept locked up in his rolltop desk a Sharpes rifle which was left at the hotel in the 1880s. More than sixty years after the traveler left the rifle in the hotel, a Missoula resident offered to buy it from Davey. Davey's response: "No deal. The man may come back for it."

As recently as 1948 the town came to life for a few hours.

Davey auctioned gold pans, harnesses, clothing, laces, high button shoes, miners' tools and other items from his store supplies, and hotel furnishings.

After the auctioneer's chant ended and the last bid was made and the many antiques bought and carted away in car and pickup, the dust settled again and with a note of finality on the hill called Chinee Grade leading to Garnet. During the 1950s efforts were made to pump out the Nancy Hanks; but by 1960, the Montana School of Mines declared profitable mining was dead. Limited tungsten mining still goes on.

Until 1970, bed springs, wheelbarrows, shovels, miners' shoes and trousers, car bodies, and twisted iron littered the landscape.

During the summer of 1970 members of the Garnet Preservation Project began restoration work on Garnet. The cooperative project included members of the Bureau of Land Management, the Montana Historical Society, the Montana University System, and the Fish and Game Department.

The J. R. Wells Hotel, Dahl's Saloon, Kelly's Bar, and the F. A. Davey's store at Garnet are among structures being restored and preserved. Ninety thousand dollars' worth of artifacts have been donated by the public as a part of the restoration project. During the summer of 1971, 15,000 persons visited Garnet.

Remains of a mill in the Garnet Mountains
—Courtesy, Ken Ring

There are five bodies buried in the Sand Park Cemetery near there. A grave robber exhumed the body of one man. When caught, he explained his actions by saying he was an antique weapon collector and had heard weapons were buried with men during pioneer times.

A few dilapidated buildings remain at Coloma.

Little is visible at Reynolds City. Twenty-six bodies are known to be buried there.

In the area around Bear Gulch, nearly 5,000 men worked the mines and streams near Beartown, Bearmouth, Yreka, Reynolds City, Top O'Deep, Springtown, Copper Cliff, Coloma, and Garnet.[4]

And among all that lies dead and dying, minds rich in Garnet-lore recall the deeds of a man who saved Garnet once, many years ago.

Snows fell up to seven feet in depth at a time, driven by bitter winds pricking the skin like needles, making a man's nose and throat hurt, inundating buildings and choking off trails.

During one winter, supply trains couldn't get to Garnet along treacherous Chinee Grade. Starvation threatened.

A man, whose name has been forgotten, saved the town. He donned a miner's light and set out through the maze of underground tunnels and mine shafts to neighboring Beartown. By road the distance was about five miles. Undergound it was eleven.

He arranged for supplies to be sent and saved the town. And his is one page in Montana ghost town lore which shines brightly in contrast to tarnished records of greed and cruelty which often permeates the history of these settlements.

Garnet will perhaps become Montana's best "non-commercial" ghost town.[5]

Of the memorabilia which typically remains at many ghost towns, remnants of working garb and tools predominate

Note the bulging walls of the hotel in Garnet

Garnet's main street, near the head of tortuous "Chinese Grade," gives some idea of what parts of one of Montana's classic ghost towns looks like today. The Bureau of Land Management plans to restore part of the town before it joins the long list of towns where too little was done too late to preserve them for future study and enjoyment

Garnet boasts many well-preserved structures, the most imposing being the hotel

Wagers had been made by many as to when the stage depot would tumble. No bets were collected, as an arsonist burned the building in 1971

When the creaking doors of the stable laboriously inch open, the visitor is greeted with a striking rear view of the hotel

1. Unconfirmed reports indicate the ball mill near Garnet was in use until 1952.
2. Former residents of Garnet tell of a properly-made bed in the hotel, which until a few years ago was left unmolested. Nature and bedding combined over the years to grow a mushroom clean through the bedding.
3. Personal interview, Pat McDonald, now of Missoula, Montana, July 13, 1972.
4. Of these camps, few physical remains are left, mostly at Garnet and Coloma.
5. For an account of Garnet lore, see John D. Ellingsen's "Garnet the Typical Ghost Town," an unpublished Montana State University thesis, Bozeman, November, 1970.

Little remains of Gilt Edge: a few stark cabins and the remains of the jail where Calamity Jane was often incarcerated

GILT EDGE: An inappropriate name.

From the beginning, mining operations in the Gilt Edge area were marginal.[1] Although some lode mining had been undertaken in the Judith Mountains beginning in 1881, it wasn't until 1893 when a cyanide mill was put in at the foot of the mountains that Gilt Edge became a settlement.

Within a few months after the Gilt Edge Mining Company began operations, payrolls could not be met. The mine manager talked with the miners. Some demanded their past-due wages. Manager

Sherard finally came up with the money and "walking papers." Having learned a bitter lesson, the remainder of the crew kept working; and when Colonel Robert A. Ammon, a lawyer from New York, took over, some more of the men received part of their back pay. The disgruntled miners asked the sheriff to issue an attachment against the bullion ready for shipment from the mine. The sheriff complied by seizing the entire plant and closing down the mine and mill. This threw the men out of work, and starvation threatened. But the sheriff distributed the several hundred dollars worth of provisions in the warehouse. In the meantime, Manager Ammon had absconded with the $25,000 in bullion. By the time the sheriff had caught up with Ammon, he was in an adjoining county where the sheriff had no jurisdiction.

Owners of the Gilt Edge mine decided to send a young lawyer, Messmore Kendall, to the scene to find out what was happening.

Kendall paid off the miners and tried to find out where Ammon was. Several months later, Ammon showed up at the mine. Ammon assured Kendall the bullion was in a safe deposit box in a Great Falls bank.

They struck out for Great Falls the next day, Christmas Eve. But the buckboard struck a chuckhole, breaking an axle. By nightfall they were lost in bitterly cold weather.

By morning, Kendall was nearly frozen. Ammon tried to get the young lawyer to his feet by kicking him. He then took his blacksnake whip, ripped off Kendall's overcoat and whipped him to keep him awake. Kendall survived, and they ultimately made the trip to Great Falls; but there was no Gilt Edge mine money in any safe deposit box in the city.

Kendall served a warrant on Ammon. There was a trial, and Ammon was found guilty. He jumped bail, and Gilt Edgers heard nothing more about him for approximately six years. When they did hear of Ammon, they were pleased. He was sentenced to five years in Sing Sing prison for his part in a stock swindle.

A five-stamp mill at the World Museum of Mining in Butte

1. The gold was known as "refractory"; it resisted ordinary methods of treatment. The gold was not "free-milling." It could not be obtained by panning or by using sluice boxes, drag lines, dredges, stamp mills, or arrastres. The cyanide process was somewhat successful, but the quality of ore around Gilt Edge was always low.

GLENDALE:

Where the charcoal odor persists.

The ruins of old charcoal kilns on Canyon Creek, near Glendale. Woodcutters chopped down trees which were burned into charcoal. Coke for power was shipped in from Pennsylvania

Southwest of Butte stood a number of towns that have disappeared or can't be reached by car. Among them were Highland City, Moosetown, Gold Hill, Red Mountain City, Greenwood, Lion City, Trapper City, and Hecla.

Remains of another town, Glendale, can still be seen. Glendale could have been named Clifton.

Both names were considered, and as so often happened in the early West, Lady Luck was called upon to make the decision. Glendale was written on one side of a wood chip, Clifton on the other. The chip was thrown over the walls of the assay office and landed with the Glendale side face up. From those beginnings, Glendale grew to a peak population of about 2,000 in 1878. The town sported a water works system and fire protection. A church was built by union subscription. It was dedicated by the Methodists. A school which could handle an enrollment of about 200 was taught by John Gannon, who later became state superintendent of education.[1]

In 1881 the Hecla Company bought the Glendale smelter, and put Henry Knippenberg in charge of the Hecla Consolidated Mining Company, which covered Hecla,[2] Glendale, Norwood, Greenwood, etc. Under Knippenberg's guidance, the operations in the area became profitable. Glendale alone probably produced between $18,000,000 and $22,000,000 worth of ore in about twenty years.

Glendale even sported a school in penmanship, conducted in a smelter office by A. F. Rice.[3]

The Hecla roaster at Glendale glowed red, the sawmill whined, the three 50-ton blast furnaces roared.

Bullion from the Glendale furnaces was moulded into bars weighing about 90 pounds each

A rare underground toilet car on display at the World Museum of Mining

A company building at Glendale

A few buildings and one stack are all that remain of Glendale

One of the few wooden structures remaining at Glendale

Charcoal and coke were used to fuel the smelters. The coke was shipped from Pennsylvania and at one time was stacked in a pile of one thousand tons. The smelter used ten tons of coke a day. Charcoal was used at the rate of more than 1,000,000 bushels a year.

Hecla operated thirty-eight charcoal kilns, fed charcoal by Italian workers who delivered it at eleven cents a bushel.

In 1882 Knippenberg located and named Greenwood, between Glendale and Hecla, and located a big concentrator there, the first concentrating mill to be erected in Montana.[4] The concentrator had a capacity of 100 tons a day.

By 1905 the Hecla operations closed, and the Glendale area died.

North of Glendale, on Canyon Creek, a dozen or so coke ovens can still be explored—all that clings to the kilns.[5]

Superintendent Knippenberg built a magnificent mansion in Glendale in 1881. It sported six fireplaces and sterling silver door knobs. It was many-gabled and had a large cupola on top. It was destroyed by fire in 1959.

Greenwood Mill. Greenwood was the site of the first concentrating mill built in Montana in 1882 (Sassman)

1. *The Dillon Tribune*, December 18, 1925.
2. According to sources in the area, mining operations were once again undertaken in 1969, but were short lived.
3. *Montana Standard*, August 20, 1967.
4. Oren Sassman, "Metal Mining in Historic Beaverhead," unpublished thesis, University of Montana, 1941, p. 244.
5. Two other kiln sites have not fared as well. One near Gardiner and one between there and Bozeman have been partially razed. The bricks reportedly make excellent fireplaces, and have been taken for use for that purpose by a number of people.

Overview of Gold Butte—Courtesy, Carl Hansen

Log cabin in front of mine entrance at Gold Butte—Courtesy, Carl Hansen

GOLD BUTTE:

Gold strike on an Indian reservation.

Indians were probably the first discoverers of gold in the Sweet Grass Hills on the Blackfeet Indian Reservation near Glacier National Park.

In the 1870s officers and men of a survey party found gold but didn't develop the area .

In 1884 a party of prospectors found gold in the Sweet Grass Hills, wintered in the area, and began working their claims the next year. They were joined by others, and ultimately a town was born in the area, called Gold Butte.

Gold Butte lived for about five years before it was added to the lengthy roster of Montana ghost towns.

GOLD CREEK:

Possibly the beginning of Montana's gold rush.

A gold rocker

Gold Creek is the center of two controversies—did a railroad spike-driving take place there, and was it the site of the first gold discovery in Montana?

John Owens was the first to record the discovery of gold in Montana in 1852. Some authorities have reported the first gold discovery in the state to have been in 1856. Francois Finlay (some say a quarter-breed, some a half-breed Indian), also called Benetsee, is often credited with finding the first gold at what is now called Gold Creek. James and Granville Stuart are sometimes credited with finding the first gold in 1862, although they had also found gold near Benetsee's find in 1859. Jesuit Father de Smet, missionary to the Flathead Indians was aware of gold in the region in the 1840s.[1]

A Historic American Buildings Survey researcher[2] claims, "Gold was first discovered in Montana in the Big Hole Basin in the spring of 1858."

It's probably safe to say the first *important placer* diggings were located July 28, 1862, on Grasshopper Creek in Beaverhead County (Bannack area), and that O. D. Farlin is credited with finding

Gold Creek has limited firefighting capability

the first quartz in Montana when he staked the Kammas lode on October 15, 1862.

A respected historian generalizes about the find thus: ". . . about 1852 . . . Benetsee found some gold nuggets at Deer Lodge Valley . . . but nothing particular happened until the enterprising Stuart brothers, James and Granville, drifted into the region from California in 1857. The Stuarts began to prospect about the Hellgate Fork of the Bitterroot, finding colors and building a sluice to garner more. They were joined by other vagrant prospectors, who helped them found the optimistically named Gold Creek Camp. Despite the camp's name, the Gold Creek sands at first gave up only three dollars in a hundred panfuls, but by the next autumn a modest quartz lode had been located. Its owners worked it with a water mill running some sort of crusher."[3]

K. Ross Toole, professor of history at the University of Montana and former director of the Montana Historical Society, feels the question may never be answered.[4]

It was *near* Gold Creek, on September 8, 1883, where Northern Pacific crews who had been laying tracks from east and west met. The driving of the interconnecting iron spike linked the first transcontinental railroad through Montana. The spike-driving by N. P. President Henry Villard is usually said to have been at the mouth of Gold Creek, but a miner who was present claims the site was at the mouth of Independence Gulch.[5]

One report seems relatively incontestable, that in 1862 the first reported hanging of a horse thief took place in Gold Creek.

For all practical purposes, the cradle of gold discovery in Montana can probably be said to have been in Gold Creek. However, the city went from the cradle to the grave rather rapidly, and today only a few structures remain; many are occupied.

A decaying dredge marks the spot where unprofitable dredging operations ceased.[6]

One aspect of the history of Gold Creek often overlooked is the fact that the infamous Bannack-Virginia City sheriff Henry Plummer made his Montana debut in Gold Creek, coming there from Elk City, Idaho.[7]

1. As respected Montana historian Dr. K. Ross Toole admits, the argument concerning who first discovered gold in Montana (and where) is likely never to be settled. K. Ross Toole, *Montana, An Uncommon Land*, University of Oklahoma Press, 1959.
2. John N. DeHaas, Jr., *HABS*, p. 130.
3. Otis E. Young, Jr., *Western Mining*, University of Oklahoma Press, Norman, 1970, p. 140.
4. Personal interview.
5. Deer Lodge *Silver State Post*, obituary of pioneer William J. Doney, March 21, 1921.
6. Until a few years ago, remains of a dredge boat could be seen just off a road leading south of Gold Creek toward Pioneer, another state ghost town. An almost intact dredge lies in a large pool of water about a half mile off the Gold Creek-Pioneer road.
7. Granville Stuart, *Forty Years on the Frontier as Seen in the Journals and Reminiscences of Granville Stuart*, edited by Paul C. Phillips. 2 vols.; Cleveland: The Arthur H. Clark Co., 1925.

Granite, where in 1889, the average silver output from the mine ran between $250,000 and $275,000 per month

GRANITE:

And the mystery of who lived on "Silk Stocking Row".

The home of Mrs. "Ma" Waring, last resident of Granite, who died at age 76. Behind the house was a mill. In the same area can be found standards for a tramway which led in the direction of the bi-metallic chloridizing, dry-crushing mill at Kirkville, later known as Clark. The two smoke stacks are all that remain of the settlement which once housed 500 mill employees

The beginnings of Granite, the "Silver Queen City," are a bit hazy.

Hector Horton first discovered silver in the general area of Granite in 1865. The Granite mine was discovered in 1872 by a prospector named Holland. But its title lapsed, and it was relocated in 1875. Holland and two friends located a claim and the entrepreneurs got a miner named McIntyre to dig a fifty-foot shaft for a quarter share of the property. When McIntyre reported the job done, the shaft was measured and found to be one foot shy. McIntyre vowed he wouldn't walk up the "damned hill" again and this rashness caused him to lose his share of the bonanza, which some have called the richest silver strike in the world.

Finally in 1880 the company which had been formed to develop the claim received financial backing from investors in Saint Louis.

Charles D. McClure, who had title to the Granite Mountain lode, struggled for two years to make the $132,000 investment pay off. McClure was certain the solid granite mass held great riches, and he doggedly kept blasting and drifting.

Arthur L. Stone, founder and long-time dean of the University of Montana School of Journalism, reports in *Following Old Trails* (pp. 274-5) that finally the day came when McClure counted his money and determined he had only enough left to pay the miners who were on shift at that time. Stone says, "It was the last shift, but the miners worked doggedly on. Through the day there had been no change in the conditions underground. The last shot was tamped home, the fuse was lighted, and the miners prepared to leave the work which they had pushed so persistently under the determined driving of the man at the head of the work. That last shot was fired. It threw bonanaz ore upon the muckers' plans . . . and Charles D. McClure became in that moment one of the greatest mining men of his time."

Before the strike was discovered, the Saint Louis backers had decided to withdraw further support; but the wire had to go from Saint Louis to either Drummond or Butte (accounts vary) and from there to the Granite Mountain mine.

There are at least two versions of the near-closing.

The vault doors of the once prosperous Granite bank hang open, revealing only the memory of better days

One claims that McClure had been notified to close the mine during the last shift, but he had allowed the men to complete the shift.

The other version is more popularly held, but not necessarily more accurate. It claims the wire was delayed in transit by a blizzard and that the messenger with the wire to stop operations met the express rider with the message that the find had been made.

In any event, between 1885 and 1892, $20,000,000 was reportedly taken out in silver and gold, enough to pay $11,000,000 in dividends and to build the large Eads (or Merchants') Bridge in Saint Louis as well as the Terminal Railway Building.

Granite prospered and in 1890 built the still-standing three-story Miner's Union Hall, which held

The Miner's Union Hall, long a center of activity in Granite, now experiences only the sound of ceiling beams crashing to the floor

Mine Superintendent Weir's residence on Magnolia Avenue, a center of controversy

a lodge main hall, meeting rooms, lounge, and recreation rooms.

Of contemporary interest is the only masonry residence in Granite, which was occupied by Thomas Weir, superintendent of the Granite Mountain Mining Company, until the silver panic in 1893.

Weir did what he could to improve the miners' working conditions. It was under his direction that a new multi-storied hospital was built. He had bunkhouses fumigated and had a "drying room" built. The drying room was meant to help keep the miners from pneumonia. They had a habit, at the end of shifts, of going outdoors with wet clothes on. Superintendent Weir's idea was to have them go to the drying room before inviting health problems caused by the sudden change in temperature. He is also credited with initiating the six-day work week at the Granite Mountain Mining Company.

Many of Granite's buildings clung to the mountain sides; the rears of many buildings were dug into the slopes, their fronts being supported by poles. The story goes that a preacher was warned not to

The Rumsey Mill—Courtesy, Montana Historical Society

pound the pulpit too hard during his exhortations for fear the two props on which part of the church rested might not stand the shock.

Until 1888 Granite residents had no piped-in city water supply. A horse-drawn cart brought in water to meet the town needs. The water came from a nearby lake, and it wasn't uncommon for subscribers to find a trout, live or dead, in the water ration.

Word came to shut down the mines in the panic of 1893. Granite became almost deserted for three years, then slowly began to regain a small percentage of its original population of 3,000 miners. But never again was Granite to be a mining center.

Today, the last resident is gone.[1] The shell of masonry of the Miner's Union Hall remains, but roof supports have fallen to the bottom floor and the third-floor dance hall, second-floor union offices, and ground-floor saloon-cafe will soon become one.

The company hospital remains, and a number of other structures, including the (perhaps) fifty-stamp mill.

Moving freight to the Granite Mine—Courtesy, Montana Historical Society

The superintendent's house is on "Magnolia Avenue," sometimes erroneously referred to as "Silk Stocking Row." Normally such a designation referred to the area in which prostitution centered. That may have been the case in Granite, too, with "cribs" for the girls near the stone structure, but Dr. John DeHaas, Jr., professor of architecture at Montana State University, believes otherwise. He says of "Silk Stocking Row": ". . . here the mine officials, doctor, and white-collar employees lived." His analysis is confirmed by a woman from Missoula, Montana, whose mother was born in the superintendent's house.

DeHaas says of the superintendent's house: "The second story under the steep gable roof may have served as an office. Access to this level was gained by a gangplank bridgeway from the uphill slope at the rear of the building. There is no inside connection between the two floors, nor has there ever been."

DeHaas is probably right in believing that Weir would not have lived in a section frequented by the girls. He had been a Presbyterian elder in Leadville, Colorado, and a member of the Theological Society at Union College in Schenectady, New York.

In a neighboring canyon is Rumsey.

It seems there was no room to build a mill in Granite, so one was constructed at Rumsey. Bricks used to build the 100-stamp mill came from Butte.

Evidence can be found of a tunnel connecting the two locations. The tunnel was blasted through the mountain between Granite and Rumsey so a narrow gauge railroad could be built to haul ore from Granite to the Rumsey mill.

Miners lived a dangerous life. Many were treated in this hospital

The five-stamp Stuart Mill, southeast of Philipsburg

1. She died in 1969 at age 75—an employee of the Philipsburg water department, she functioned as a ditch rider.

HASSEL:

Dead and gone.

Hassel was originally known as Saint Louis.[2] Placer ground was discovered on Indian Creek,[3] near Hassel, as early as 1866, and during its active mining years the creek grossed about $5,000,000 in gold.

Although placer mining petered out by about 1880, at various times before and after 1880, stamp mills were operating, and some dredging operations went on.

Tom Reece owned the Jawbone gold property near Indian Creek and needed a stamp mill. He made a deal with a freighter to haul one from Fort Benton. Reece was another of the frontier's entrepreneurs of no mean talent. The tale goes he loaned $1,000,000 to mining magnate F. Augustus Heinze.

It's reported that in the fall of 1896 the nonpartisan Hassel Independent Silver Club was founded in the interest of silver and the election of William Jennings Bryan.[4]

The settlement has disappeared. Gaunt, sheer canyon walls silently stare on the townsite in a wasteland of classic rattlesnake country.

A flume still clings to the mountainside near Indian Creek below Hassel

2. Exactly when the name was changed is unknown. Up to near the middle 1890s, the name was Saint Louis. By 1895 the name had been changed to Hassel, in honor of Joseph H. Hassel, a pioneer miner. Wolle, *Montana Paydirt*, p. 130.
3. Near Indian Creek Hog 'em, Beat 'em or Rob 'em (as some called it) on the flats of Indian Creek lasted a very short time. Cheat 'em was three miles west of Hog 'em, reports the *Townsend Star*, April 9, 1964.
4. Wolle, *Montana Pay Dirt*, p. 130. In 1896 Bryan was nominated for president by the Democratic National Convention, the People's party and the Free-Silver Republicans. The platform espoused the free coinage of U.S. silver at the ratio of 16-to-1. William McKinley defeated Bryan by 600,000 votes.

HELENA:

Where gold still lies upon and below Last Chance Gulch.

It was July 14, 1864. Uncle John Cowan, John Crab, D. J. Miller and Reginald (Bob) Stanely (possibly Stanley)[1] had been prospecting. They were on their way to winter in Alder Gulch, but decided on the way to pan a creek in the Prickly Pear valley. Because of the lateness of the season, this would be their last chance to prospect the area before heading west. They sank two prospect holes and struck it rich. The gulch was appropriately named Last Chance Gulch.

As the gulch began to fill with others seeking instant riches, the miners decided they must come up with a name for the mushrooming town. From such possibilities as Pumkinville, Squashtown, Cowan, Stanely, Wood, Tomahawk, Tomah, and Saint Helena, the miners decided on Helena, perhaps after Saint Helena, Minnesota. The Minnesota town was pronounced Saint HeLEENA. To the miners'

A contrast of old and new at Alhambra

Remains of cyanide tanks at an unnamed camp near Helena
—Courtesy, Marco DeAlvardo

way of thinking, HEL may have spelled "Hell," and Helena was called HELena. One theory claims "Helena" was chosen because it meant "a place far in the interior."[2] Others say the city was named in honor of a lady.[3]

Within about four years, $7,000,000 in gold and silver-lead deposits had been wrenched from Last Chance Gulch. Most of the metals were free-milling, and several mills were built to crush and treat the ore.

By midsummer 1865, three thousand people were crowded into narrow Last Chance Gulch, digging prospect holes and shafts down to bedrock. Many buildings were undermined as the search for gold went madly on. "A dancehall girl at the Gayety Saloon, newly arrived in town, stepped to the back of the hall where she worked to get a breath of air between whirls. She opened the door and stepped off into space, landing shaken and bruised on bedrock, ten feet below. Only that day the ground under the building had been excavated and the hall propped up."[4]

Helena's main street was built along Last Chance Gulch, and even today when "gully-washers"[5] come along, the torrents of water wash down gold, some of which settles in the streets. The Placer Hotel, along the gulch, was largely financed from gold taken from the gravel which was excavated for the foundation. Reports have it that for down-and-outers, it's more profitable to pan gold than panhandle along Helena's Last Chance Gulch.[6]

Near Helena are several sites where miners once

toiled. Among them are: Alhambra, Silver City, Scratch Gravel, Gregory, Blackfoot City,[7] Unionville, Elliston,[8] Montana City, Clancy, Woodville, White's City, Emery, Avon, Park City, Dry Grass, Springville, Corbin, Wickes, and Diamond City. Most have disappeared.

Corbin, Wickes, and Jefferson City still live. Notable about Clancy is the fact that placer and lode deposits near it caused the town to grow until about 1880. In 1879, the first woolen mill in Montana was established there, but that venture, along with mining activities, was short-lived.

Gould, near Stemple Pass between Helena and Lincoln, is virtually inaccessible by car. There are some structures remaining at Stemple, on the pass which bears its name.

A Forest Service sign is all that marks the site of Diamond City,[9] which once had a population of perhaps ten thousand. The yield from the ravine at Diamond City was between ten and twelve million dollars.

Unionville once boasted a population of several thousand, and before it was added to the long list of Montana ghost towns, it had its day in the sun. Some of the mining scenes for the movie "The Growler Girl" were filmed there in 1926. About the only vestige of mining days remaining is a stamp mill.

Avon, a distribution center for many towns in the area, still exists. Old-timers are fond of recounting how the entire town was terrorized for two days. A supposedly trained bear gave a performance in front of the Cramer House, then decided to have a look-see at Avon.

For two days the trainer tried to capture the bear, while Avon's citizens quaked behind locked doors. What finally ended the crisis was a bottle of whiskey. As the bruin guzzled booze, the trainer captured him.

Mining operations still go on at Wickes, for this was metal-rich country. The Alta mine alone produced $32,000,000 in silver and gold. At least three fires ravaged the town in the early 1900s, and little remains today. Dumps and tailings abound and the ruins of smelters and refiners and coke ovens still stand. There's an abundance of steel balls from the old ball mill, used in the ore-pulverizing process.

The *Roundup* (Montana) *Tribune*[10] maintains that with their twenty-two saloons and five dance halls, the 1,500 souls of Wickes created such a litter that "cards strewed the main street so thickly that for several years a man with a team was hired to clear the street every morning."

A few buildings remain at Blackfoot City. One is occupied by a Butte miner who occasionally works his hardrock mine.

After romping in Montana for several years, Calamity Jane finally came to rest in Mt. Moriah Cemetery, Deadwood, South Dakota

Here, the tales go, a prospecting party found a $3,000 gold nugget in Deadwood Gulch; and at Pence's Discovery, a group of miners used a nugget worth $11,880 for a handball.[11] In nearby McClellan Gulch was "Whiskey Keg Store," a large whiskey keg converted to a store.

"Mining magnate William A. Clark figures into the history of Blackfoot City. Clark was a merchant in Bannack during the winter of 1866-67 when a shortage of tobacco occurred in Blackfoot City. Clark made the round trip of about 500 miles in biting cold weather with a wagonload of tobacco, and made a profit of about 300 percent."[12]

Residents had their troubles with Indians, murderers, claim jumpers, and camels!

George T. Wickes, a New York contractor and mining engineer, for whom the town of Wickes was named—Courtesy, Montana Historical Society

A ghostly, deserted Blackfoot City cabin. The table is set for a meal, but the last supper was eaten here years ago

In 1854 Secretary of War Davis decided to conduct an experiment to determine if African camels might prove to be appropriate beasts-of-burden for American military operations. Two years later nine dromedaries, twenty-three camels, one calf, six Arab attendants, and a Turkish camel veterinarian began testing the abilities of the animals in a new environment. The camels performed admirably, carrying 1,000 pounds of supplies and ores—about twice the amount mules could. Also they found their own forage and ate food a mule would reject. The Department of War brought over 41 more, with plans to import an additional 1,000.

But for a variety of reasons (one of them that mules and horses stampeded when they saw camels), the beasts didn't work out very well, and at the end of the Civil War all were offered for sale.

A freighter bought a camel pack for his Montana run. One day while they were grazing, a Blackfoot City resident named McNear, formerly of Missouri, mistook a grazing camel for a moose. With visions of fresh meat on the table, he took aim with his rifle and fired. Perhaps because McNear was an "easterner," Blackfoot Citians claimed his shot was pure luck. In any event, he brought the camel down.

The freighter didn't take too kindly to the mistake, and McNear's rifle, ammunition, money (reportedly $300), watch, and deed to his mining claim in Ophir Gulch changed hands in payment for the miscue. In addition, the Missourian was ordered to dig a grave for the camel.

About a mile from the site of Blackfoot City is an interesting graveyard. It squats, fenced in, high in a pasture along the mountainside. Calamity Jane[13] maintained her mother was buried in Blackfoot City, but her marker is not in the graveyard.

The waterwheel used for running an electric generator at Blackfoot City

This sign is all that remains at Diamond City

A Butte copper miner, who works his own Blackfoot City claim on weekends and vacations

1. There is general agreement that Cowan and Stanely were original discoverers. However, Crab and Miller may not have been involved; rather it may have been Cabe Johnson.
2. Davis, *Shallow Diggin's*, p. 123.
3. *Ibid.*
4. Wolle, *Montana Pay Dirt*, p. 71.
5. Water from heavy rains which rush down into the gulch are termed "gully washers."
6. Davis, p. 127.
7. Also called Ophir.
8. Elliston operated to supply cordwood for Marcus Daly's smelter in Anaconda.
9. The site was located on Confederate Gulch, so named for two Confederate soldiers, Washington Baker and Pomp Dennis. Nearby Montana bar, though covering less than two acres, was a rich strike; often yields of up to $1,000 a pan were reportedly taken. One clean-up is supposed to have yielded more than $1,000,000 in gold.
10. November 24, 1927.
11. Another report says a miner was playing catch with a nugget worth $1,880, in *The Grass Range Review*, November 28, 1938.
12. Greever, *The Bonanza West*, p. 223.
13. Facts concerning Calamity Jane and her relatives are difficult to get at. One area of current concern and controversy is whether the enigmatic female had a daughter.

KENDALL:

And the saga of gold, chicken houses, cattle and boy scouts.

He had been a successful Lewiston-area rancher before learning mining in the Spotted Horse and Maginnis mines near Maiden. He also owned a boardinghouse-restaurant in Kendall before the gold bug hit him. And though there had been prospecting and some mining[1] in the area before he came, probably no one was as successful as Harry T. Kendall. By 1900 he had built a cyanide mill, a house, a stable, and a boardinghouse for his forty employees. That summer, utilizing a cyanide process, the Kendall Gold Mining Company was making an average of $800 a day. In the first five years of its operation, $2,500,000 of bullion was wrested from the earth.

The gold at Kendall was extremely fine—so fine it was often not visible to the naked eye. Kendall was one of the first camps to use the cyanide process to separate the gold from unwanted materials. The ore was first crushed into small pieces, then mixed with a sodium cyanide solution. Zinc shavings (or dust) were added to the mixture as a precipitate. The sludge was put into a large burner or roaster. By this intense-heating method, the zinc was driven off, and the gold remained.

An interesting tale of Kendall evolves around the discovery of "The Gopher Hole."

A prospector, Joe Wonderland, on his way home, sat down to rest. He saw a gopher hole, scooped up a handful of earth around the hole and took the sample to the assay office in White Sulphur Springs.

The assayer wasn't in his office, so Wonderland left the sample on a desk in the assay office, along with a note with the words "gopher hole."

After the assayer had evaluated the sample, he asked the prospector where he picked it up. The miner told him, and some say this is how a nearby mountain came to be called the Gopher Hole.

Men drilled 300 feet into that mountain and 800 feet around it to get to the gold.

In 1902 and 1903, many structures were built in Kendall. Perhaps the most imposing was the Shaules Hotel, a 26-bedroom,[2] fireproof, two-story structure with hot water, hot-air heating, and electricity.

Kendall was booming: it had two churches, a blacksmith shop, Jones' Opera House, several saloons, Turner's Mercantile, the bank-lodge hall, a post office, and four stagecoach lines. And to top it all, on March 25, 1902, the *Kendall Chronicle* announced that soon there would be a self-propelled vehicle called a "locomobile" connecting Kendall and Harlowtown, about 75 miles distant, and the time of journey would be but a few hours. John R. Cook, the hustler for Kendall, "planned to have the vehicle built." It would be operated by steam, powered by gasoline (reportedly less than two gallons would be consumed on the trip). "It . . . shall have a carrying capacity of 4,000 pounds, and as many as 16 passengers will find accommodations." The two-car vehicle would have "four-inch solid rubber tires. This breadth of tire will help to solve the problem of traveling over roads in muddy condition." Top speed was expected to be 12 miles an hour.[3]

Kendall never received its locomobile.

Among Kendall's citizens was a lawyer named "Fat Jack."

Although nothing of substance could be proven, the consensus was that Fat Jack cheated clients. Finally, the tale goes, sufficient numbers of people

Stage leaving Kendall about 1903—Courtesy, Montana Historical Society

Kendall Hotel between 1900 and 1910—Courtesy, Montana Historical Society

in the Kendall area banded together to have a "necktie party" with Fat Jack the "honored" guest.

An eyewitness to the hanging says, "Three or four men pulled up on the rope and let him down. It took four tries before they successfully killed him."

The men retired to their favorite haunt—a saloon.

Within minutes Fat Jack strolled in and bought the house a round of drinks. Although the 300-pound attorney could hold his booze, he finally staggered home to bed.

The undaunted "hanging crew" came up with the idea of detonating several sticks of dynamite under Fat Jack's cabin to do what the hangman's noose had failed to do.

The dynamite blew the house apart, but not Fat Jack, who promptly returned to take up drinking where he had left off.

Ultimately, through a grand jury investigation, the necktie party was found out, partially through the efforts of jury foreman Dave Hilger (the town of Hilger was named for him). Apparently Fat Jack held no grudges, and didn't press charges against his would-be killers.[4]

Road agents always kept a sharp eye and an alert ear out for gold shipments. They were sometimes successful, sometimes foiled, in their efforts to pick up easy money. On one occasion the wife of a miner used $30,000 of gold bricks as a footrest on the trip to the bank in Lewiston. A stage driver once brought what was ostensibly two kegs of nails to Lewiston; the kegs held money.

In yet another instance, a stage driver for a $50,000 shipment was told to take the money to Lewiston's Brown's Clothing Store instead of the bank as a diversionary tactic. Brown, being busy waiting on a customer, asked the driver to put the money bag on the counter, promising that he would put it in the safe later. Somehow Brown forgot about the money bag and left the gold on the counter at closing time. Word had leaked out that there was a gold shipment at Brown's. Assuming the money was in the safe, thieves blew it open. They found only $200, overlooking the gunny sack of gold which was still on the counter.

Kendall's population reached 1,500; between nine and fifteen million dollars worth of precious metals was dug from its mine.

Then, in 1920, the Barnes-King Development Company closed. The town died. "Down from the canyon where the noise of a thriving town had been came wagons loaded with everything from children to building materials. The houses were drawn on skids to become dwelling or hen houses of ranchers in the valley. Silence descended upon the mountains."[5]

Today, three stone foundations remain in Kendall, a gazebo, and a pocked porphyry boulder—a permanent reminder of old-time drilling contests.

Parts of some of the town can be found on area ranches. Some of the buildings collapsed because mine shafts beneath them sank, bringing down buildings with them. At present, a large herd of Black Angus and Hereford cattle share the lonely site with Boy Scouts.[6]

A double jack drill team on Miner's Union Day in Kendall, June 13, 1910—Courtesy, Montana Historical Society

Harry T. Kendall—Courtesy MHS

Kendall's Wedge Saloon, 1903—Courtesy, Montana Historical Society

1. Lambert Florin, in *Ghost Town Album*, Superior Publishing Company, Seattle, 1962, p. 169, says, "The first really good mine at Kendall was the Goggle Eye, so named from the way the discoverers looked at the first sight of the gold.
2. Jean Davis, in *Shallow Diggin's*, estimates there were 40 rooms in the hotel.
3. *Kendall Chronicle*, March 25, 1902.
4. This tale was recounted by an elderly, one-time resident of Kendall. He wished to remain anonymous.
5. *Great Falls Tribune*, July 14, 1935.
6. In recent years, Boy Scout troops have utilized the town site for a camp. A new bandstand built for their use stands in marked contrast to the ghostly remains of what was Kendall.

The life and death of Pike Landusky are interwoven with the story of the life and near-death of Landusky, Montana.

Indians knew of gold in the Little Rockies long before the young, fresh-from-Missouri Powell Landusky got off the steamboat at Fort Benton in 1864.

By the time he arrived at Last Chance Gulch, little, if any, good placer ground was left. So the gangly, quarrelsome six-footer took on a job as a freighter. He held the job for two years before heading down the Missouri to the area near the mouth of the Musselshell with a partner, John Wirt. They planned to trap and wolf.[1]

That fall, Landusky and Wirt had trapped about $800 worth of furs and pelts. They cached it away and headed for Carroll for supplies and fun.

During their absence, a Brule Sioux war party relieved them of their furs, pelts, camping equipment, and almost every other worldly possession.

The same band took the two trappers prisoner on their return. That evening, the Sioux gave the white men some buffalo meat, which Landusky began to cook. One of the braves decided he'd rather take Landusky's meat than prepare some. "Thereupon Landusky flew into one of his uncontrollable fits of passion. Seizing the heavy frying pan, he struck the Indian over the head with it, splattering him with grease. Then grabbing his gun, he poked it into the Indian's stomach and knocked him down. He then seized the Indian by the breechcloth, pulled it off and whipped him over the head and face with it. This was the worst insult he could offer an Indian warrior."[2]

The fight went on, with Wirt coolly standing by, the loaded rifle lying over his arm.

". . . while the Sioux were hurrying over from their camp, one of the warriors pointed to Landusky and made the sign for 'crazy man.' He believed (and very reasonably so) that only a man without his senses would take such chances. This explanation of Pike's ungovernable rage was accepted by the remainder of the Sioux; and as all plains Indians were possessed of a superstitious fear regarding a crazy person, and as it is against their medicine and religious beliefs to harm a person so afflicted, they immediately caught up their horses and fled."[3]

This was neither the first nor the last of Pike's encounters with Indians. One winter Pike and partner "Flopping Bill" were trading whiskey to the Indians. One day three Sioux strolled in, and Pike recognized two of them as being among those who had stolen from him the previous winter. In another of his typical rages, Pike quickly killed two and ran after the third with an ax. He caught up with the unfortunate Indian, hacked him to pieces, scalped the three bodies and threw them through a hole in

The final resting place of the violent lad from Pike County, Missouri: Powell, "Pike" Landusky

LANDUSKY:

It still lives near the shadow of the weathered grave marker of its founder.

Landusky's, where "Pike" Landusky and Kid Curry had a showdown

Remains on the edge of a huge settling pond at Barker

the river ice. This episode ended the Pike Landusky-Flopping Bill partnership, but not Pike's hate for Indians. The story is he hired out to local stockmen for $20 per Indian scalp, and carried with him a tobacco pouch made from the bladder of one of his Indian prey.

Although he hated Indians, Pike knew trade with them could be lucrative. He and Joe Hamilton (and probably John J. Healy or possibly a man named Boucher) set up a trading post on Flatwillow Creek in 1880. It wasn't long before Pike was having altercations with his customers.

Pike claimed a young brave tried to stab him in the back. Landusky knocked down the Indian and hurled chunks of wood at him. Nobody knows what happened, but moments later two Indians came out of the post bleeding from head lacerations.[5] Partner Hamilton came along and barred the trading post door on Pike, telling him to cool off.

Hamilton then tried his powers of conciliation in a parley with the Indians. It was working until one of the bloodied Indians broke the small window on the post with a sapling.

This brought Landusky, with a Winchester in hand, head and shoulder protruding from the window. Pike blasted away at the Indian with three shots, which missed. The Indian's partner shot at Landusky, shattering his right jawbone. Landusky reloaded and shot the squaw of the Indian White Calf. Moments later another Piegan bullet ripped into his body.

Friends carried Pike to the bunk, where he fell into another of his frequent fits of anger. He grabbed his mouth with his fingers, tearing off part of his jawbone, with four teeth attached.

Accounts differ as to how Pike was "doctored up." In one version, it is said it took a week for his partners to get him to Lewiston to Dr. LaPalme, during which time Pike lived exclusively on whiskey.[6] The other story is that one of the white men rode to Fort Maginnis to fetch an unnamed army physician. The doctor set the jawbone and dressed

Pike's wounds, then returned to the fort. According to that account, "For ten days there was no apparent improvement; so Dr. DePalm [*sic*] was summoned from Reed's fort [Lewiston]. . . . Dr. DePalm decided that the jaw had been set wrong and that it would be necessary to rebreak it and set it again."[7] Pike gave the go-ahead, and the second surgery was a success, although his face was disfigured for the rest of his life.

After a slow medical recovery, Landusky and Hamilton moved to Maiden, where they set up a saloon. Pike married a widow who had seven children. Their marriage is reported to have been the first in the recently-opened boom camp. Three years later Landusky went to the Little Rockies in search of gold. He and Dutch Louis Meyers found it in Little Alder Gulch. Pike discovered the first lode mine in the area, then a second, a third, and ultimately had staked at least thirty claims.

The settlement of Landusky was organized on June 9, 1894. It soon became a favorite hangout for gunmen, claim jumpers, murderers, robbers, rustlers, and assorted unsavory characters.

Among those attracted to the area were the Curry (previously called Logan) brothers.[8] Harvey, Henry, Johnny, and Loney. The Curry brothers located at the mouth of Rock Creek, and were neighbors of Pike Landusky.[9]

The Currys and the Landuskys got along well for several years.

However, in 1892, a feud developed.[10] Pike was mighty sore at the entire Curry gang, but had a chance to vent his anger only on Harvey, nicknamed "Kid," and brother John. The Currys had been arrested for altering a brand. Pike was deputy sheriff, and during the short time the Currys were incarcerated, is reported to have chained them to the wall of the jail and beaten them up. The brothers were released because of lack of evidence and were bent on getting even with Landusky.

It was nearing Christmas time, and the town was looking forward to a big celebration. At a town meeting, it was decided that as something special for the occasion, the townspeople would have four dozen quarts of Baltimore select oysters. "Orders were given to 'Lousy' the stage driver, to wire for them when he went to the railroad. Lousy had never bought any but cove oysters before so he wired to Minneapolis for them, thinking the oyster beds were at the foot of the falls of Minnehaha. The express on them was more than the original cost of the oysters.

"From that time until the big day the camp was all feverish activity. The big time was all the topic of conversation and fully a barrel of bourbon was licked up in considering details and devising new features.

Monarch, jumping off place for Barker and Hughesville

Barker, where on one cold January evening, several residents went to a neighboring camp's masquerade ball ". . . as God made them and appeared fittingly for the occasion"

One of Neihart's livery and feed stables

Word had gone over all that sparsely settled country that Landusky was entertaining; they all heard it and they all came. . . . They drifted in from the badlands 60 miles away, from grassy valleys in the foothills, from the alkali flats farther out, from remote places in the river breaks and from the gulches of far reaches of the mountains. They came in all the vehicles that were known to the time and they brought food enough to feed the multitude in the wilderness, those who didn't get a break on the loaves and fishes."[11]

About 100 people showed up for the Landusky Christmas celebration. And as expected, the oysters were the culinary highlight. "It wouldn't do to let a novice monkey with these bivalves, they had to be prepared and served by a chef who knew how. So 'Tie Up George' the most famous of all roundup cooks, was drafted into service and warned not to get cocked up until the feed was over."[12]

"Tie Up" did right well by the oysters; an organ was brought in from ten miles away. Johnny Curry loaned his new barn for the dance, while Loney led the home talent orchestra. They danced, drank, and ate for two days and two nights.

"Yet there was a tenseness through all of this apparent gaiety that seemed to forebode a tragic ending. When the gun fighters first came to town they all discarded their guns for the time being. If they wanted to wake the echoes for a moment they'd borrow a gun from the barkeep and have at it. The day following Christmas, in the evening, they all rearmed and everybody clung close to his arsenal. Every man there was watching, he didn't know just what for! The second morning after Christmas, Dec. 27, it came—as all had known it would come eventually."[13]

It was clear to most that something might precipitate the Curry-Landusky feud.

The morning of December 27, 1894 was frosty and white. It was warm in Jew Jake's Saloon. (Pike had built the saloon-mercantile store.) Pike and Jew Jake (Jake Harris) were friends. Jew Jake had come to Landusky *via* Great Falls. He had lost a leg in a gunfight with the city marshal. As usual, Jew Jake was hobbling around. Sometimes he used a crutch, sometimes a sawed-off shotgun for support.

It wasn't unusual for Pike to come into the saloon at midmorning, but those who had stayed over from the Christmas blast knew that something unusual might happen. It did.

Within three minutes of Pike's arrival, Kid Curry made his entrance.[14] He slapped Landusky on the back (or shoulder, versions vary),[15] and as Pike looked to see who had delivered the blow, he was met with knuckles to the jaw. At gunpoint, onlookers warned those in the saloon not to interfere with the proceedings.

Landusky, knocked to the floor, was pinned down by The Kid and badly beaten. A friend of Pike's cried out to end the fight. Nobody heeded the plea, and Pike's face was soon a bloody mess. The Kid kept hammering away at Landusky until his head and face looked "almost like a black eye."[16]

When Kid Curry was certain he had beaten Landusky into submission, he let up and was surprised to see Pike rise and, like quicksilver, draw his gun. However, "It was one of the new fangled automatics that had just come out at that time, and either Pike didn't know how to use it or it went wrong. . . . Anyway, it didn't work. The Kid found himself in a moment, drew his .45 and it was all over. He shot Pike twice in the head—and missed the third time—and Pike battled no more."[17]

Pike was buried on his ranch, a half mile from Landusky; while Kid Curry headed hastily toward his native Missouri.[18] The Kid joined a gang headed by Butch Cassidy and the Sundance Kid. A report that he was buried near Landusky appears to be erroneous. He was almost apprehended in Knoxville,

Hughesville, the sister city of Barker, on a cloudy, rainy afternoon

Lehigh, which supplied coal to nearby camps

Tennessee, but escaped, many believe to South America.[19]

Pike's remains were officially recorded as Powell Landusky. Five other graves flank the Landusky marker.

Although Kid Curry's final resting place is in doubt, that of brother John is not. He and his "lady friend," a recent widow, rode out to see her deceased husband's partner. Their idea was simple: convince the man that she should receive, along with John, title to half of her husband's ranch. Jim (or Ike) Winters didn't agree, and delivered a fatal broadside gun blast at John Curry. His marker is in the Landusky cemetery.

Loney finally gained the affections of one of Pike's stepdaughters, and lived with her in common law marriage in Landusky. However, he beat a hasty retreat back to Missouri when his "wife" tried to pass a bill in a Fort Benton store, identified as one from a recent robbery. Pinkerton men caught up with him near Kansas City and put a bullet in his head.

Today, few in Landusky recall the days of Powell Landusky, killed in 1894. But many remember the not-too-long-ago days when Landusky was a thriving mining town. They listen to the sounds of the Canadian company exploring the mountains above the town for whatever minerals they can find. They persist in their "friendly" rivalry[20] with neighboring Zortman and are excited by the arrival of "the stage," bringing news, mail, and groceries from Zortman and the outside world.

Windham, a supply, transportation and recreation center for area miners

A not uncommon business combination in the old west

1. "Wolfers" usually placed buffalo meat on the prairies, to which had been added a generous helping of strychnine. Shortly after the wolves ate the poisoned meat, they were ready to be skinned.
2. *Kalispell Times*, September 23, 1920.
3. *Ibid.*
4. Lewiston *News-Argus*, December 17, 1972.
5. They were White Calf and Running Rabbit.
6. Wolle, *Montana Pay Dirt*, p. 372.
7. Davis, *Shallow Diggin's*, p. 272.
8. No explanation is given why the Curry Brothers had previously gone by the last name of Logan. Dorothy Johnson, in *Western Badmen*, Dodd Mead, 1970, p. 222, says this was one way to keep from being identified.
9. They also owned mining property adjacent to Landusky's ranch.
10. The feud may have developed over a borrowed plow, or Pike's refusal to let one of his stepdaughters return the attentions of Loney Curry. What seems most likely is that daughter Elfie probably came to Pike and told him he was about to become the grandfather of Loney's son.
11. John B. Ritch, *Great Falls Tribune*, January 20, 1935.
12. *Ibid.*
13. *Ibid.*
14. A slightly different version is given by James D. Horan in *Desperate Men*, Bonanza, New York, 1969, pp. 198-9.
15. One fairly recent newspaper account (1936) indicates Curry didn't even bother with a hand on the back or shoulder, but rather struck Landusky with a heavy blow to the face.
16. *Great Falls Tribune*, January 20, 1935.
17. *Ibid.*
18. Lambert Florin, *Ghost Town Treasures*, Superior Publishing Company, Seattle, 1965, p. 82. The battle still rages, but credence is given to the theory that Curry was in reality a man known as Tap Duncan, now buried in the churchyard in Glendale Springs, Colorado.
19. Still another report is that seven years after the fight Curry held up a Great Northern passenger train at Exeter Siding west of Malta and carried $80,000 into the hills (Toole, *Montana, An Uncommon Land*, p. 249).
20. While residents of both towns are apparently relieved that Zortman and Landusky still survive, citizens of each make claims and counterclaims about their respective historical significance, weather, general living conditions, etc., etc.

LAURIN:

Where two of Henry Plummer's gang were strung up.

Two large log barns are reminiscent of Dewey's earlier days, when hundreds came for the 4th of July celebrations, including, but not limited to, drinking, square dancing and horse racing

The fortunes of Laurin were intertwined with those of Virginia City, Bannack, and Alder. Laurin, as a supply center near Alder Gulch, shared in the $100,000,000 riches of the gulch.[1]

Much of the history of Laurin (sometimes called Cicero, sometimes Lorrain) is built around the Frenchman, Jean Baptiste Laurin, who ran a trading post along the route.

M. Laurin began operation of his store in 1863. He was only five feet, seven inches tall; some reports estimate his weight at near 350 pounds. Although he could neither read nor write, he was a shrewd businessman, and one estimate is that he built an economic empire valued at about $500,000. One report indicates that at one time he owned ". . . all the stores, bridges, and most of the ranches, cattle, horses, and mules for fifty or one hundred miles along the valley."[2] His herds were reported to be scattered over four valleys, ". . . and his stores are found in every settlement, with their supplies of canned fruits and vegetables, groceries, a few dry goods, a profusion of prepared cocktails, bitters, etc., and every variety of robes and skins."[3]

M. Laurin was also a money-lender, charging anywhere from twelve to thirty-six percent for unsecured loans.

Perhaps the most interesting structure left in Laurin is the Saint Mary's Assumption Church. Father Joseph Giorda, S.J., head of the missions in the Rocky Mountains, was serving in Virginia City when a theatre building was remodelled in 1865 to serve as All Saints Church. The following year, the church received a bell which Father Giorda had purchased in Saint Louis and had shipped up the Missouri River to Fort Benton, then hauled to Virginia City by wagon. The 400-pound brass bell was cast in 1848. In 1930, when the Virginia City church was razed, Virginia Citians began to attend the Saint Mary's Assumption Church, built in Laurin in 1901. The congregation brought the bell with them to their new church, where it still stands.

1. Size and production considered, Alder Gulch ranks as the world's richest placer gulch. Much of the profits went to Harvard University, whose equipment once operated on the stream bed. Miles of tailings between Alder and Virginia City attest to the riches taken from the area.
2. A. K. McClure, *Three Thousand Miles Through the Rocky Mountains*, Philadelphia, J. B. Lippincott, 1869, 311-12.
3. *Ibid.*

Laurin, where two of Henry Plummer's road agents were hanged

Cattle now roam the site of Kendall, which is a Boy Scout camp. The 40-room stone Shaules Hotel, Jones' Opera House and many of Kendall's best structures were used as chicken house foundations on nearby farms. The bandstand is a granary

LITTLE BELT CAMPS

Several former mining camps and supply centers, in or near the Little Belt Mountains south and east of Great Falls, are a part of the state's mining history.

Windham existed primarily as a supply center for miners from Lehigh and Utica. It was named for a town in Vermont from which its founders had come.

At its peak, 1918-1920, Windham had a newspaper, a livery stable and barn, bank, pool hall, and two saloons.

Much of the atmosphere and memorabilia of the turn of the century can be found in such places as Duncan Gillespie's general store and drug store. Gillespie, who in 1970 was honored as Montana's oldest pharmacist, knows the history of the area well. Indicative of the atmosphere in his mercantile store is a poster advertising a well-known laxative—dated 1907.

The road to nearby Lehigh is good, having been built on an old railroad bed.[1] They were mining coal, rather than metals, in Lehigh, beginning in 1914. By 1920 the weekly payroll was $75,000 for the 300 miners, mostly Poles and Finns. Eighteen hundred people lived at Lehigh; the grade and high schools had 815 children enrolled at the peak of operation. When the Lehigh coal mine closed, most of the buildings were burned, torn down, or moved to Stanford.

Also in the region is Utica, a minor gold camp during the early 1900s.

Utica was overshadowed by Hughesville and Barker. Patrick Hughes and "Buck" Barker were prospecting in the Little Belt Mountains. On October 20, 1879, while Barker went hunting, Hughes located a strike. Hughes named the mine for his sidekick, and a town was born near the site. Hughesville was later located a half mile east of Barker.[2] By 1880 the area's population approached 100.

A smelter was built at Barker to handle the silver-lead ore from the mines which had sprung up in the area. It closed in 1883 after one-and-one-half years of operation.

In 1891, a branch of the Great Northern railroad was completed to Barker, and hopes mounted that ore could profitably be shipped to the Great Falls silver smelter. Some of the first passengers on the new train were members of the Great Falls Bicycle Club. After a four-hour visit to some mines near Barker, all but two got back on the train. Captain Matteson and Mr. Mitchell had brought

their bikes along and decided to cycle to Monarch, twelve miles away, and catch the train there. They took off ". . . at a speed that should have caused the locomotive to blush with humiliation."[3] According to a newspaper report, "The excursion party was made up of the elite of Great Falls, and represented the best class of society that Montana or the world affords."[4]

News of rich strikes near Neihart siphoned off most of the population of the area. The last edition of the Barker newspaper was printed in 1894, lamenting the fact that the town could no longer support a newspaper.[5]

In the summer of 1881 several miners, including James Neihardt, left Barker and found silver in a gulch near present-day Neihart.[6]

The population of Neihart alternately expanded and contracted according to the mining activity of the moment.[7] One of the booms came with the completion of rail connections to Great Falls in 1891. Passengers from Great Falls were joined by some from Helena in making the fifteen-mile-an-hour Great Falls-to-Neihart excursion. But it was mid-November, and the Neihart Free Coinage Brass Band found it impossible to offer a musical welcome to the visitors—it was too cold. Dynamite blasts were set off in the nearby mountains, a silver spike was driven, souvenir badges were handed out; and then because of the biting cold, most visitors headed for Neihart's saloons.

As a consequence of the abbreviated program and the elongated saloon visitations for "Tangle-leg,"[8] the return trip was jovial, until Jew Jake (Jake Harris) tangled with Great Falls Marshal George Treat.

Repeatedly, on the trip, Treat tried to get Jake to be quiet. Jake began to call the marshal names. When the train drew up to the Great Falls depot, the area was cleared rapidly. The passengers knew there would be a showdown. Jew Jake waited on the platform as Marshal Treat, the last to leave the coach, stepped down.

Jake was the first to fire, but his aim was wild and he hit and injured a bystander. The marshal fired, bringing Jake to the platform, shot in the leg.

The limb was amputated, and Jew Jake, realizing his welcome in Great Falls had worn thin, headed for Landusky. He operated a saloon there, hobbling around using either a Winchester or sawed-off shotgun as a crutch.

One of three remaining blacksmith shops in Hobson

1. It was fairly common, when the railroad no longer found operations profitable, to tear up tracks and use them elsewhere. Often motor roads were built on these railroad beds.
2. During its early existence, ore from Hughesville was hauled by bull team to Fort Benton, then down the Missouri and Mississippi rivers to New Orleans and transferred to ocean steamers for shipment to smelters at Swansea, Wales.
3. *Belt Mountain Miner*, September 23, 1891.
4. *Ibid.*
5. *Ibid.*, January 27, 1894.
6. Neihart was named for James L. Neihardt, uncle of poet John G. Neihardt.
7. Approximately forty mines have been operated in the vicinity. As an example of Neihart's "expansion-contraction," even today, within the city limits of Neihart can be found ruins of a former town, Jericho.
8. Whiskey. Also called "Red Eye," "Forty-rod," "Rot Gut," "Lightening," "Tarantula-juice," and a variety of other names.

MAIDEN:

"Fondly courted... heart broken they withdrew".

Maiden about 1900—Courtesy, Montana Historical Society

"Oh, Maiden, beautifully fair,
Couched between those mountain hollows,
Charming thy form and golden hair
And eyes bright as silver dollars.
Maiden of wealth on paper told,
Breast of pearls, ribbed with silver,
Awaiting ready to unfold
And give up her rarest treasure.
Maiden whom many anxious sought,
Fondly courted, strived to woo;
Who to empty words heeded not,
Smiled while heart broken they withdrew."[1]

So went the poem about Maiden, appearing in the *Rocky Mountain Husbandman*, July 27, 1882. Earlier the same month, the same mining camp was referred to in the *Benton Weekly Record* as Maidenville. But the confusion begins even earlier than that. Montana lore says even the mountains in which Maiden rested were misnamed. The legend says Meriwether Lewis, of the Lewis and Clark expedition, wanted to name a mountain chain after a girl back home. Apparently Lewis was better at recalling faces than names when he dubbed the Judith Mountains. The lady's name was Julia.

There are at least three accounts of how Maiden was named. In one version, Mrs. James H. Connely asked two prospectors who were going to establish

The Central Montana Junior Chamber of Commerce has placed signs and published maps and a brief history of Maiden so the visitor can identify various sites and buildings

a townsite at the present location of Maiden, northeast of Lewiston, what they would call the place. They were going to name it after a squaw named Grovenire. They asked Mrs. Connely what she would call the site. Mrs. Connely replied that since the prospectors called her daughter "Little Maiden," they might name the town after her.

The second version says that when a man named Maden came to the area, he was informed everything was staked, but he could move on up the gulch. Maden moved on to another gulch which he named after himself. He put up the sign, "Camp Maden. Everybody welcome." That location became the town center, the word "Camp" was deleted, and "i" was added.[2]

The third version is that the place was called Maiden because it was so inaccessible.[3]

The first prospectors in the area were "Skookum Joe" Anderson and Dave Jones in 1880. The pair came up with an interesting device resembling a sluice box. They split trees into troughs and placed clay in the bottom of each trough. They ran the gravel through the V-shaped apparatus. Gold, being nineteen times heavier than water, sank to the bottom. The clay-gold combination was removed, and the gold separated from the clay.

By 1883, there were 154 houses and stores in town.[4] And that was the year Maiden was almost abolished. On August 8th, under orders from Captain Cass Durham, commanding officer of the cavalry battalion stationed at nearby Fort Maginnis, all residents were ordered to leave in sixty days. Since Maiden was within the military reservation[5] the order was a valid one.

The aroused citizens formed a committee; they drew up a petition, which was presented to Captain Durham. Since Durham's orders had come from higher up in the chain of command, he felt he had to follow through as long as Maiden remained within the military reservation. But he did not object to a slight adjustment in the reservation's boundaries, and Maiden returned to a normal routine. In following years, thefts of cattle and horses by Indians increased, but at least the town was saved.

"Justice" passed from the hands of the military to the citizens. In 1886, about thirty citizens decided five Chinamen were no longer desired in Maiden. Although the group had posted skulls and crossbones in several conspicuous places, the "celestials" didn't take the hint. The thirty donned masks and visited Gee R. Joe, the laundryman on Montana Street. He was advised "that the hour of his departure had arrived and any unnecessary delay would not be conducive to Longevity."[6] He was joined by four others who were "escorted" a way down the gulch, and told to keep going.

Although $18,000,000 in gold was mined, milling activity dropped. In 1888 the population was 1,200.[7] In 1896 it had dwindled to 200. Many structures were moved to Lewiston, some to Kendall. A fire in 1905 virtually destroyed the town. There was no reason to rebuild.

The Spotted Horse Mine in Chicago Gulch, above Maiden

The Maginnis Mine and Mill at Maiden—Courtesy, Montana Historical Society

The first funeral held in Maiden, 1883
—Courtesy, Montana Historical Society

Much of the brew made at Landt's Brewery—the first in the state—was consumed at Gie's Saloon

The remains of Belanger's Department Store. Belanger's private cemetery plot is on a knoll, a short distance north of the store

1. *Richland County Ledger*, January 9, 1922.
2. Florin, *Ghost Town Album*, p. 163.
3. Davis, *Shallow Diggin's*, p. 248.
4. The first commercially manufactured furniture probably arrived in Maiden in 1885 *via* oxen team.
5. It would appear the military reservation was there before Maiden was founded. Whether the incursion of Maiden was inadvertent is unclear. C. C. Snow and J. R. Kemper laid out the townsite. But the land had not been surveyed, and neither title nor deed could be given for lots. As soon as one purchased a lot, he showed possession by fencing his property.
6. *Mineral Argus*, January 14, 1886.
7. An influx of miners came briefly, after Perry McAdow exhibited a gold and silver statue of the actress Ada Rehan at the 1893 World's Fair in Chicago.

MAMMOTH:

A misnomer.

Most of the original structures of Mammoth have been converted into summer homes. This one is an exception

Signs at both ends of Mammoth's one street warn the traveler to drive slowly; there are children at play. And occasionally, during the summer months, there are, in this town south of Whitehall.

In the mid-1950s, the town was sold, and the new owner "developed" the site—in a way. It's now used as a summer cottage site, mostly for residents of Butte.

Portions of structures were torn down and attached to others to make fairly sturdy and habitable cabins. The nights are cool, for the town is more than a mile high. McGovern Creek sometimes floods the road—but life appears pleasant.

Remnants of earlier mining activities scar the area. The biggest producer was the Mammoth mine. Much of the mill remains. More than $14,000,000 in silver and gold came from Mammoth-area mines. Remains of the tramway from the mine down toward the town are still visible.

Redesigned Mammoth is hardly a ghost town today.

Bank vault at Mammoth

MARYSVILLE:

Including Thomas Cruse, Montana's Horatio Alger.

A back-alley scene at Marysville

Marysville in the 1890's—Courtesy, Montana Historical Society

Marysville is another of the not-quite-ghost towns of Montana. The last official census lists the population at forty; residents place it at closer to seventy-five. In any event, there aren't enough students to keep the grade school open, although it has recently been remodelled, and is still used as a voting place; the Methodist church has closed. The Catholic church is still operating, and a general store serves most of the needs of those left, of a city which in the 80s and 90s was Montana's leading gold producer and boasted a population of up to 50,000.

Many structures remain in Marysville, notably the brick and stone buildings which served as the Masonic hall, drugstore, post office, grocery store, hotel, and saloon. In the saloon near the bank the tables, booths, and fixtures still look much as they did when the establishment was operating.

Much of the lore of Marysville centers on the luck of one Irishman, "Irish Tommy" Cruse. At first the young, inexperienced Cruse always returned with nothing but an empty poke and a smile that got him another grubstake. Cruse had a friend in nearby Helena who let him sleep on his drug store counter when Tommy lacked the wherewithal to get better accommodations—which was almost always.

Finally, near the present site of Marysville, Irish Tommy hit it rich. He named the mine the Drumlummon, after his birthplace in Ireland; and he founded Marysville. Some say Marysville was named after the first three Marys who lived there. Others

The famed Drumlummon Mine near Marysville, burned down shortly after this photo was taken in 1971

say it was named for Mary Ralston, the first woman there. Still others say Mary was the name of the woman who was grubstaking Tommy when he discovered the Drumlummon.

In any event, the town grew; and Irish Tommy, in a period of six years, netted almost $150,000 in bullion. Authorities estimate the total production from the Drumlummon (which recently burned to the ground) to be $50,000,000. During the 1880s and 1890s, Marysville appears to have been the state's leading gold producer.

Irish Tommy finally sold the mine for $1,500,000 to an English syndicate.

He moved to the capital of Helena, rode in a carriage, lived in fine surroundings, helped build a cathedral, founded a bank, and was generally unhappy. He bought the Bald Mountain and West Belmont mines near Marysville and was happy again. He saw his former mine, the Drumlummon, mismanaged.

Muriel Sibell Wolle, in *The Bonanza Trail*, recounts:

> The English company which bought the Drumlummon spent fortunes on the mine. Many of the stockholders were English aristocrats whose sons were sent to the mines to become engineers or mining experts. They were paid large salaries and were well housed. At one time there were more officials than miners! The company provided electric lights, steam heat, and hot and cold water to

The Drumlummon Mill—Courtesy, Montana Historical Society

A saloon scene in Marysville in 1911. The saloon was operated by Lehman and Thoenes (or Thones). One of the owners, Charie Thoenes, is tending bar—Courtesy, Montana Historical Society

Many a Marysville youth sought to practice his pitching on the windows of the Methodist Church, rather than the deserted ball diamond

The Marysville Methodist Church, where never again will service or hymn be heard

Structures on Marysville Main Street

the officials' homes and furnished them lavishly. The grounds of the manager's house were landscaped by a trained gardner, and even the pump station resembled a Gothic chapel. When the company needed a new pump in 1890, they ordered a Cornish one at a cost of $55,000, paying an additional $33,000 in freighting costs. They sent for an expert from London to install it. The water in the mine was so low when he examined the property that he scornfully remarked that there wasn't enough water even to prime the pump, and hurried back home. Nevertheless, the pump was on its way. While it was being hauled up the canyon, however, the wagons carrying it broke down, the pump rolled into the bottom of the gulch, and the company never bothered to retrieve it. No wonder the firm went broke.[1]

Nor did another mining entrepreneur fare as well as Cruse. Nathan Vestal took $80,000 and a 242-pound bar worth $54,262.62, and sold the mine for $400,000. Vestal had a hankering to return to the East and enjoy life, including card playing, which he did. He even spent a year savoring the joys of Europe.

Many in Marysville were surprised when Vestal wired a friend for money to buy a ticket back to town; all were flabbergasted when he arrived in Marysville and began working at his own mill for miner's wages of $3.50 a day.[2]

Thomas Cruse never went broke, living a long and prosperous life in Helena. He was generous, but not in all instances. He was asked to donate two lots for a Catholic church in Marysville, but didn't

The umpire's call to "play ball" will never be heard again

Six teachers once held classes in this Marysville school. Recently, the top floor was removed, the structure reroofed and stuccoed in white

like the idea. Finally, he was convinced that he could part with one lot; but somehow, when the edifice was completed, it occupied the *two* lots otiginally asked for.

Although Irish Tommy came to be referred to as Mr. Cruse and learned to write his name, though not to read, similar refinement didn't come to the citizens of Marysville.

There were the girls from "silk stocking row" if a man had the money. There was a straight shot of whiskey or a "whiskey-ditch" (whiskey with water) or a beer. And there was Lady Luck.

She could make the cold sweat flow and the gut tighten. She could dry the throat, make the hands tremble and the palms sweat and the heart pound. She could make a man whoop and holler and buy the house a round, or crawl home penniless or in debt.

There's no reason to believe Marysville had more or less gambling than other towns, but there are more people left in Marysville to tell about it than in most "ghost towns."

The tram from one of the mines had a weak section. As the ore cars came down the tracks, the miners would bet on whether it would make it all the way down without overturning. There's the tale of one of the "girls" who decided to end it all by drowning herself in a pond. The jump coincided with a shift change at the mine. While the bets were hastily offered and called as to the girl's fate, one of the miners jumped into the mill pond to rescue her—whereupon bets were made on him, too.

The general store is a good place to hear tales of Marysville, especially those about 4th of July celebrations which lasted for several days. This was the social highlight of the year. The fights were numerous, the inebriates could be counted by the hundreds. Thousands of gambling dollars changed hands.

The celebrations of the Chinese added an oriental flavor to Marysville. Their incantations aimed at driving away evil spirits were an annoyance to some citizens, but on a lesser scale than the Chinese food offered to the spirits: small white mice dipped in honey.

Southwest of Marysville are a few cabins at Gold Butte. Nearby Belmont's three or four cabins remain as mute testimony of livelier days.

Northwest of Marysville are remains of Stemple (on Stemple Pass) and Gould.

1. Wolle, *The Bonanza Trail*, p. 197.
2. *Ibid.*, p. 198.

The Marysville Catholic Church, which "Irish Tommy" helped build, almost in spite of himself

View from a hill overlooking Marysville

This portrait of Dimple Blackiston, taken in 1899, is typical of portrait work on the Montana mining frontier—Courtesy, Montana Historical Society

Marysville on a late autumn afternoon

The stable at the Mystery Camp

MONTANA'S MYSTERY CAMP

The huge mill at Montana's Mystery Town

Montana's mystery camp was perhaps named in honor of an American president. Remains of what may have been the last narrow gauge railroad to be built in the nation are there.

A tornado sucked up huge trees, heavy boulders, everything in its path, creating a desolate half-mile-wide swath on the outskirts of town.

A well-preserved mill—probably the state's largest—still clings to the side of a mountain, and a couple dozen structures stand on what is perhaps the Treasure State's least-desecrated ghost town main street.

It hasn't been restored. No efforts have been made to preserve it except indirectly—for those who know of its existence refuse to give out information about it. They fear this historic place will be desecrated by man. Odds are excellent they are correct.

Of the dozen or so outhouses at the Mystery Town, not one remains standing, suggesting that perhaps Halloween pranksters were at work

Mystery Camp hotel or boarding house

A Mystery Camp structure, probably built by Scandinavians

A mystery in Mystery Town. The intended function is a matter of speculation

This lone, crude cross stands in the Mystery Town

NEW CHICAGO:

It joined Montana's Brooklyn and New York-- unable to equal or surpass their eastern namesakes.

Large green signs on Highway 10A point to New Chicago, but the town is no longer in existence. A pasture is the site of the former town, and buildings have been moved to other locations for varied uses

In 1872, a town was born on the Mullan Road south of Drummond, called New Chicago. Its founders were certain it would rival and ultimately overtake its Illinois namesake because of its strategic location as a trade and transportation center.

In addition to stores and the inevitable saloons, there were blacksmith shops, a flour mill, and a livery stable. There was a school at New Chicago too, for pupils who ran the gamut from "6 years to 6 feet."

Fourteen years after the settlement was founded, an Epsom salts container was placed in the Methodist Episcopal church cornerstone. It held various church-related items, newspapers, a nickel, and a twist of tobacco.

Most of the anecdotes of New Chicago revolve around Mr. and Mrs. Dennis Mitten. Sobriety was not one of their virtues, and they were probably not present during the laying of the church cornerstone.

One day the lady of the cabin was in Bear Gulch, and hearing of impending Nez Perce raids, fortified herself with a needle gun[1] and a bottle of spirits. After spending a few hours in close order drill in the Gulch and commanding herself to fire spasmodically at the flags adorning the stockade fort, Mrs. Mitten somehow found her way home to the ranch.

Dennis, burdened with such domestic duties as doing the chores and "fixin' vittles," wasn't in the best of moods when his spouse finally maneuvered her portly frame into the ranch house.

Dennis was understandably concerned about his wife's performance in Bear, and a family discussion ensued. Dennis made the almost fatal mistake of asking his wife what she would do if he were one of the raiding Indians. She retorted that she would aim and fire her weapon, which she did—at Dennis.

The Indians didn't come, and Dennis survived; perhaps the wiser for the encounter, he made the prudent move of setting up a saloon to meet the needs of the Northern Pacific construction crews who were laying track through town.

One evening Dennis and a workman had a misunderstanding. Dennis grabbed for his wife's gun and chased the workman through the brush. When the railroader reached a nearby river and began to swim across, Dennis in frustration fired once at his escaping quarry.

About a month later, when the body was found, Dennis Mitten registered surprise at being told that he had fired the fatal shot. He was arrested and sentenced to seventeen years in the state penitentiary in Deer Lodge .

It didn't hurt Dennis' cause that the prison warden was his wife's nephew, and he soon was pardoned. But this was not to be his last brush with the law.

Mr. Mitten's triumphant return home was due cause for rejoicing. He and his wife rode up to New Chicago where all their friends joined in the gay celebration. Everybody congratulated them and voiced their hearty welcome by setting up drinks. Consequently, by evening the whole town was in a drunken uproar, with the Mittens, to each of whom the passing years had added many pounds, the natural center of the festivities. Everyone was happy, although few, at this final stage, could doubtless have explained the primal reason for their happiness. At last the reunited couple, having sung and shouted and laughed themselves hoarse, decided to go home. Kind hands helped them onto their horses where they perched unsteadily. As a parting token a generous bartender gave them each a bottle of whiskey. The whole town stood watching them ride out of sight up the canyon, swaying perilously in their saddles.

For the sombre finale to that gay day of reunion we have only Dennis Mitten's heart-broken confession. It was very cold, he said, and there was about four inches of snow on the ground. When they had traveled within a mile of their ranch, Mrs. Mitten, who had been seeking warmth and comfort from her bottle all the way, toppled off her horse and lay in the snow in a drunken stupor. Dennis was in a serious predicament. It was impossible for any one man to lift the huge, limp woman back into her saddle. To leave her in the snow while he went for help meant she would freeze to death. And so, after his liquor-befogged brain had puzzled over the difficulty for some time, the worried husband hit upon a plan which seemed to him a logical answer to his problem. He tied a rope around his wife, secured it to the horn of her saddle, and then, mounting his own horse, led hers home, with Mrs. Mitten dragging through the snow behind. When he arrived at the ranch he hastened to release his wife and discovered, to his sorrow and deep grief, that she was dead.

And simple Dennis Mitten, who had bungled all his life, was again charged with murder. He was tried, convicted and sentenced to return to Deer Lodge where he died.[2]

Today, many original New Chicago structures from the town predicted to rival "old Chicago" have been requisitioned for contemporary uses, such as storage areas for farm produce and animal husbandry purposes.

Probably New Chicago died a victim of more efficient means of transportation developed in the early 1900s.

1. A primitive breech-loading bolt-action rifle.
2. *Kalispell Times*, August 6, 1936.

Early day photo of a sluice operation

An arrastre—Courtesy, Sassman

PARROT:

Some parrots talk--not this one.

Now known as Parrot, the town was originally named Gaylord, for Jared E. Gaylord, one-time manager and superintendent of the short-lived mining operations.

Tales which can be neither proved nor disproved, graying records, and intrigue surround the history of this town on the banks of the Jefferson River, south of Whitehall.

Even though the long steel bridge, the sole access to the site, has been washed out for years, remains of a smelter are discernible from across the wide Jefferson River.

Today, by road or on foot, it's difficult to even know if the large, two-story red brick house, which was designed to serve as the smelter office, exists.

Sagebrush hides the kiln, built in 1896 by a Butte firm.

From newspaper reports, it would appear that prior to 1895 the Parrot smelter was located in Butte. The January 4, 1895 issue of the *Jefferson Valley Zephyr* says, "For a year or two there has been talk of the removal of the Parrot smelter from Butte to a point five miles south of Whitehall on the Jefferson River" (the approximate location of the present Parrot smelter). The article continues, "R. D. Grant, asst. gen'l. Manager of the Parrot Co. said recently to an *Anaconda Standard* reporter: 'We have been keeping very quiet and doing a little pardonable lying relative to the contemplated removal'."

Apparently the 1,000-ton plant was completed, at a cost of several million dollars. Parrot grew up near the smelter.

A later newspaper article, this one from the *Grass Range Review* of December 17, 1917, reports: "About the time the smelter was completed the Amalgamated Copper Co. was formed. The big company absorbed the majority of the Parrot Mining Co. stock, and the ores of the Parrot went to Anaconda, where the big smelting plant of the Anaconda Co. was located."[1]

The Gaylord smelter was never operated. After a few years of idleness, its machinery, which could not be used by the larger company, was sold for junk.

Seeking bedrock

A Chinese pump

1. One report indicates the Parrot smelter was operated by Copper King William Andrews Clark of the Colorado and Montana Smelting Company: *see* Carl B. Glasscock, *The War of the Copper Kings*, The Bobbs-Merrill Company, Indianapolis and New York, 1935, p. 89.

THE PHILIPSBURG AREA

Where gold was often found at the "grass roots".

The Gold Coin Mill. Gold was found in pockets in the area, then "glory-holed" and milled in this structure

The area around Philipsburg was, and still is, rich with precious materials.

Philipsburg was named after the inventor of square-set mine timbering. With him, Philip Deidesheimer also brought the knowledge of the "pan amalgamation" system used in Nevada. The system was so successful in Montana that a town was named after him, but since use of his surname would have meant calling the settlement the unwieldy Deidesheimerburg, his first name was used. Philipsburg was often referred to just as "The Burg."

Philipsburg became a trading center for the various nearby settlements. Its population rose to about 1,500 in the mid-60s, but dwindled to three in 1869. By 1873 many deserted mines were reopened, and the town once again began to grow. Today, its population has stabilized at about 1,000.

The Gold Coin mill near Philipsburg stands, near collapse, as an example of what happens when gold is found at the "grass roots."

In order to get to the gold, which was almost on the surface, the miners dug into the earth, then

Red Lion

Typical cabin at Princeton

Remains of the waterwheel which powered the Stuart Mill near the banks of Georgetown Lake

drove a drift back toward the surface. Much of the gold was so close to "grass roots" that today tree roots can be observed growing into the mine.

For a time W. J. White owned the Gold Coin mill. He invested profits in the Yucatan Chewing Gum Company and became known as "Chewing Gum White."[1]

The area around Princeton, northeast of Philipsburg, was the site of limited and generally unprofitable mining activity. Several occupied cabins dot the townsite.

The towns of Tower[2] and Hasmark grew up very close to Philipsburg. Being only a half-mile apart, the two towns virtually grew into one. The mine which appeared to have been worked over the longest period of time was the Algonquin. The Algonquin mill ultimately boasted a total of eighty stamps. Both silver and gold were taken from the mine, which closed in 1883. In the early 1900s, apparently, the mine, or one of the same name close to it, reopened. Zinc, lead, and silver manganese dioxide (used in the manufacture of dry cell batteries) were mined. At its peak there were about 150 men employed at the Algonquin, which was closed in 1968. Today, on the other side of the mountain, in the Limestone mining area, two men are still mining.

A couple of cabins and some summer homes are all that remain of "Old Georgetown," a short-lived mining camp founded in 1868, which twnety years or so later was a ghost town.

Southern Cross is yet another Philipsburg-area ghost town of interest. In 1969 the boardinghouse was razed; the post office was earlier crushed by a falling tree. Several company buildings covered with sheet metal remain in various states of disrepair. The Anaconda Company now owns the mine properties. They have fenced off the area, and "no trespassing" signs are liberally sprinkled throughout the site.

Like Southern Cross, Red Lion is close to the 7,000-foot level, and travel to the site is often confined to the months of July and August and part of September. High snowdrifts in late June are not uncommon. Various forms of vegetation are reclaiming the site of Red Lion.

Remains of an arrastre are on Flint Creek, below the location of the former Red Lion mill. The

Boarding house at Cable. Miners were almost forced to eat here, as "board" was withheld from their salaries

arrastre was run by power generated by a fourteen- to sixteen-foot high, four-foot-wide water wheel, the buckets of which were tongue-in-groove, five-quarter lumber.

The Atlantic Cable mine and the camp of Cable City were located in 1866 or 1867 by three men. The mine commemorated the laying of the second trans-Atlantic cable. Some say two of the three discoverers were sailors who had worked on the laying of that cable.

The Nowlan mill was built to process the Atlantic Cable ore. It's reported to have been the third mill to be built in Montana Territory.[3]

The town grew to a peak population of about 350.

Some erroneously believe the world's largest nugget, supposedly worth $10,000,[4] came from the Atlantic Cable quartz lode in 1889. A cigar box worth of samples was frequently reported to be worth $1,000, and several gold nuggets valued at several thousand dollars were found. The Atlantic Cable quartz lode was so rich a 500-foot area reportedly produced $6,500,000 in gold. Some gold was so pure twenty-one pound ingot was displayed at the New Orleans Exposition, and some Cable gold was shown at the Centennial Exposition. Cable became

Gold Coin Mill near Phillipsburg

Company building at Southern Cross

Mining machinery used at Combination Mine near Black Pine

Boarding house at Southern Cross

so famous the Post Office Department put out a commemorative stamp.

Although the Cable mine was the largest producer, others in the area of major importance were the Hold Fast, Hidden Lake, and Red Lion. About 150 men worked at the Cable mine. Perhaps upwards to 500 Chinese were employed in various mining operations in the district.

It's rumored that there is a street called "Cable Terrace"[5] in Great Britain, lined with fine homes which were financed by ore stolen from Cable.[6]

Some miners attempted to sneak out gold in their clothes, but the mining company superintendent sealed off that avenue of high-grading. He made the men change clothes after they came off shift. But the wily miners came up with an alternative plan. By burrowing into timber, they found they could stuff gold into these holes, and throw the timber over an ore dump, where their wives would just happen to be gathering firewood—and timber with gold inside!

The Cable mine has been opened and closed several times. At this writing, the area is being worked again, with the mining crews living in trailer houses. A building housing a compressor is there, too. That is about all that remains at Cable. The bulldozer and torch of the present developer have done their jobs well. Even the weathervane and birdhouse which were atop the front of the barn pictured in this chapter are now gone. In 1971 the barn still stood, as did the schoolhouse. But the autumn of 1969 was disastrous for Cable. At least seven cabins were destroyed, joining the assay office, the mill, blacksmith shop, Diamond Head core storage shed, and the combination general mine office, warehouse, post office, and assay office. Months before, during the winter of 1968-69, snowmobilers had burned down the ten-room, two-story boardinghouse.

Feelings of ill-will are expressed against the present developer by some ghost town buffs, for he was also apparently responsible for burning down virtually all that remained of yet another ghost town —Black Pine. Others maintain in a free enterprise society he has every right to do as he chooses. And the thought persists in the area that probably only about one-half the riches of the Cable area have been uncovered, and someone should find them.

While some mining towns had no graveyards, and many had one, Cable had three. One was reserved for miners. Another contains a marker of the child of the mine manager. The headstone depicts shoes and socks, as if thrown to the floor by a child on his way to bed. The third contains the bones of the "bandit" of Cable—a Chinaman who was full-time cook and part-time highwayman.

This, and other publications contain reports of how the Chinese were discriminated against. Histories of mining towns reflect the first birth of a "white" child, never that of a Chinese or Negro. Hundreds of incidents are recorded, perhaps thousands are unrecorded, of injustices perpetrated against minority groups.

It was a common event to set out a plot for a graveyard, and if no whites cooperated in its habitation, Chinese were killed to "seed" the plot. The Chinaman's wages were usually about 50 cents a day, as opposed to $3.00 a day for his white counterpart. The "Celestials" often worked ground thought "petered out" by their white counterparts, often at no great profit, but still it was "pay dirt."

Throughout the written histories and the accounts of miners, only two accounts of some kindly gestures toward Chinese emerged. One was that of Chinese John, who lived near Superior. He toiled long and hard and was rewarded with limited funds and a more lengthy life than might have been expected in the difficult frontier existence. Before he approached the century mark, perhaps the oriental was not in full possession of all his mental facilities. As miners passed his way, many would stop to see if he needed provisions from Superior stores. John had few worldly possessions, but would give his friends a pittance of money and ask that they bring back certain supplies. Often what he gave them covered only a fraction of the actual cost of the goods, but somehow the difference was made up. These accounts are unofficial, but often recounted by persons in the Superior area.

The only written account uncovered was in the *Belt Mountain Miner* in 1892 and 1893 regarding incidents in Barker. It seems that "John the Chinaman" was a good firefighter in Barker as early as 1892. John, the sole Chinaman in town, was also known as Ah Lee. The Chinese were usually harassed; so when John left town for a few days, both he and the white citizens were surprised that nothing had been disturbed but the sign on his laundry. The sign was returned, and "Last Thursday was the Chinese New Years and John . . . celebrated it in great style. He kept a good supply of Chinese and American liquores and other Chinese refreshments[7]

Miner's clothing left years ago at deserted Red Lion

on tap and all his friends and customers were invited in to share in the good things."[8]

A Forest Service sign, a shed, and a hoist mark the present site of Black Pine. Down the road, parts of the mill at Combination remain. Otherwise, there are very few remnants to mark the location of two Philipsburg-area camps which once had a population of about 1,200.

The years 1882-1890 were the most successful for the two camps.

Early mining was centered on the Combination vein. By 1887 a ten-stamp mill was in operation, but by autumn the company was in debt. Stockholders refused to put more money into the operation. Litigation followed, and in September the county sheriff closed the mill. The Combination and Black Pine Company's holdings were auctioned off, but some of the original stockholders were certain the operation could become a paying one. They bought the properties back under the name of Combination Mining and Milling Company. By the next spring operations were in full swing, at a profit.

Like many company towns, Black Pine and Combination were relatively sedate.[9] Company policy would not allow saloons or honkytonks inside the city limits. But there were some who needed a bit of recreation after a hard day in the mines, so "Whiskey Hill" was created a couple of miles from the outskirts of Black Pine. Saloons and brothels flourished in what may have been one of Montana's first "suburbs."

Water was about as expensive as whiskey, and perhaps not as tasty for some. A horse-drawn cart hauled water into town, valued on the average at one dollar per gallon.[10]

Much can often be learned about a ghost town through an examination of its cemetery. But Black Pine didn't have one—its dead were buried in Philipsburg, eleven miles away.

A disastrous forest fire in 1889 burned out the Black Pine mine hoist and about fifty buildings. Today, Black Pine and Combination are, like hundreds of other Montana ghost towns, mere shadows of the past.

One of several sauna bath houses in Cable. Most Finnlanders in Cable had a sauna

A wooden flume still carries precious water to the site of Tower

Although visitors are not welcome, several scenes in Southern Cross can be photographed

1. Florence Riddle Johnson, *Ghost Trails Country*, privately printed, 1964, p. 32.
2. The settlement was also known as Troutville.
3. Florence Johnson, p. 13.
4. Another estimate is that the value of the nugget was $19,000. Most authorities seem to feel the world's largest nugget was the Welcome Stranger, found at Ballart, Australia. The 2,280-ounce nugget has been valued at $42,000. Another report that a $200,000 nugget was turned up at Breckenridge, Colorado, appears suspect.
5. Florence Johnson, p. 16, says it's "Cable Road."
6. This is unconfirmed.
7. What the *Belt Mountain Miner* reported in July 13, 1892, and February 23, 1893, respectively, regarding "refreshments" and "good things" may have included drugs, in addition to Chinese culinary delicacies.
8. *Ibid.*
9. Relatively quiet mining towns were avoided by many, the feeling apparently being that no self-respecting miner would locate in a one- or two-saloon town if he could help it.
10. Prices for water varied—being highest in late summer, when supply was shortest.

PIONEER:

The town that was literally ripped apart.

The only reasonably intact building left in Pioneer, a town virtually smothered in piles of tailings

Most mining states had a town named Pioneer, and Montana is no exception. Actually, Montana had *two* Pioneers. The first has disappeared; the second will shortly.

The saga of Pioneer #1 is a variation on a common mining town theme: population up to 4,000; $20,000,000 in placer gold coaxed from the gulch.

The frustrations of life in a mining camp are aptly captured by Jean Davis in *Shallow Diggin's* when she quotes the following poem from a bartender published in the *Missoula and Cedar Creek Pioneer* on April 27, 1871:

Take pity, Miss Fanny
The Belle of Pioneer
And grant some indulgence
To a vendor of beer
Whose heart rending anguish
Will bring on decline
Oh, God of creation,
I wish you was mine.
We'd live in a parlor
Behind the saloon
With sour-krout [*sic*] *in plenty*
For our honeymoons;
We'd have schnapps by the bottle
To make it go down
And live in more splendor
Than any in town.
There is Fowler and Fischer
And Wallace of yore
There's cows and there's chickens
And many things more
But none like your Perry
That sells lager beer
His tender heart is breaking
Each day in Pioneer.

. . . .

So now my dear Fanny
If you will incline
To join me in wedlock
Just drop me a line
And great expectations
With me you will share
Not to mention the sour-krout [*sic*]
And oceans of beer.
PIONEER CITY, April 24th, 1871

Author Davis also reports on a "doodle bug[1] expert," Gus Wisner:

The "doodle-bug" according to Wisner is similar to the "water witch." It is based on the theory that all metals give off electrical waves of magnetism. These waves, from certain metal in the ground, attract waves of a similar metal on the surface and cause a definite reaction.

When the "doodle-bug" operator wishes to find gold bearing ore, he makes a gold "doodle-bug." This is done by placing a small piece of gold in the top of a small wooden triangle measuring about an inch on each side. Two holes are bored at each end of the base of the triangle and into these are forced two willow sticks, or handles, about three feet long.

As rays from gold run north and south, the operator faces north and grasps the willow handles at their extremities. He holds the "doodle-bug" parallel to the surface and the palms of his hands are held upward, with the thumbs turned out. The fingers are lightly closed around the willow handles, but not tightly enough to impede its movement.

The operator walks north. When gold below the surface attracts, through its magnetic waves, the metal in the "doodle-bug," the instrument is slowly forced up without the aid of the operator's hands.

Mr. Wisner claims his is an infallible method of locating all kinds of metal. . . .

As for the operation of the "doodle-bug" only people of a certain type have the natural qualifications necessary for the "doodle-bug's" successful operation. One must have a certain amount of electricity in his body. . . .[2]

The first Pioneer was taken over by the Gold Creek Mining Company, Ltd. when placer operations were no longer profitable. The English company began dredging operations. Later it sold out to Patrick Wall. Wall and his wife may have been two of the first western "urban planners." They tore down the first Pioneer and built a new one. The Walls were not motivated by any particular desire to improve the quality of life in Pioneer. Rather, the old buildings were sitting on top of rich gravel, and they wanted to get to the gold.

So they built a hotel and dance hall, presumably on already-worked land. Cabins for miners were planned which were copies of Yukon cabins. A few were built.

Remains of dredges, one wooden structure, and remains of three rock buildings are all that remain of the second Pioneer. The area is unmarked, fenced in, the extensive piles of tailings more resembling the surface of the moon than Mother Earth, with the result that Pioneer is perhaps the most ugly example of degradation in Montana mining town history.

Apparently most structures were dynamited by the cattleman who owns the town site. Reportedly, cattle occasionally fell through the floors of the decaying buildings, sometimes breaking their legs.

1. The stick used in divining was commonly referred to as a "dowser stick."
2. Sid Stoddard for the *Lima Ledger*, April 25, 1932.

POLARIS

A former bright star in the Big Sky.

The present site of Polaris, northwest of Dillon, is two miles south of the original townsite. The smelter and cabins located at the original camp are gone. The boardinghouse was moved to the present site and today functions as a store and post office. That structure, a shed, and the Polar Bar tavern are all that remain of "New Polaris."

The Polaris mine was located in the Lost Cloud (sometimes referred to as the Beaverhead) mining district. Although the Silver Fissure mine produced silver in 1886, the Polaris mine was the most important silver lode in the region. It was located by six men on January 31, 1885.

In 1892 the mine changed hands and was later bonded and leased in 1900. The Polaris mine was purchased again, this time in 1905. The buyers, the Silver Fissure Mining Company, built a smelter near the mine and used steam traction engines to haul ore over the forty miles of wagon road between the mine and Armstead, a town now under water, formerly on the Oregon Short Line Railroad. (Near the turn of the century six-horse teams hauled the ore to Dillon for shipment.) A 100-ton smelter with four blast furnaces was erected near the mine in 1906-1907. A fire destroyed most of the smelter in 1922; but it made little difference, for the mine was only operated until 1908.

Astronomers know of Polaris as the star Alpha Ursae Minoris (or the Little Bear), and also as the North Star, Polestar, and Cynosure. The people in and around Polaris, Montana may or may not bother to watch Polaris, the bright star at the tip of the tail of Ursa Minor, but they surely closely watch the post office-store and saloon business to help gauge when may come the almost inevitable death spasms of Polaris, Montana.

Polaris camp and smelter. The 100-ton smelter was built in 1906-1907. Fire destroyed most of the smelter in 1922—Courtesy, Sassman

A "secret" clubhouse near Polaris

The store and post office at Polaris. Across the street in the tavern, is the bar brought from Bannack, where Henry Plummer reportedly had his last drink

The site of recently abandoned mining operations north of Polaris

PONY

And that is why the Post Office called PONY, MONTANA is now in Madison County instead of Fergus County

A Chilean Mill, which was probably developed from the arrastre. It consists of a single stone roller running on a stone pavement, powered by horse or water wheel. Ore is ground on a Chilean Mill until it is fine enough to add mercury, then it is ground again, until panning indicates that all the free gold is amalgamated. This mill is on display at the World Museum of Mining in Butte

There are "one-horse towns" in Montana, but there are also two "Pony" towns—one in Fergus County, one in Madison County.

The first to be established was in Fergus County. The town was named for Pony McPhartland who owned a trading post. Inside the trading post was the post office which Pony ran, not for profit, but for the convenience of the people in the area. It's reported that on the average he made only about $6 a year commission selling stamps.

The *Hardin Tribune Herald* of February 13, 1937, recreated an incident which had earlier erased the Fergus County town from the maps and postal registers:

One day a stranger rode up in front of the store, alighted from his cayuse and tied it to the hitch pole.

Pony [McPhartland], seated on a bench just outside the door, greeted the newcomer with the simple hospitality of the west. The fellow immediately developed an attitude of inquisitiveness, however, that jarred upon Pony's sensibilities.

"Where's the postoffice?" he asked abruptly. "That's it," said Pony, pointing to a five-gallon kerosene can with the top cut out of it that stood on a shelf just inside the door.

Just then a resident of the neighborhood rode up, dismounted, dropped the reins of his horse, and with a brief greeting to Pony and the stranger,

Morris State Bank in Pony, Madison County, Montana

stepped through the door and helped himself to the contents of the can.

He examined each letter attentively. . . . He ran on through the pile of letters, showing an intimate knowledge of the affairs of everyone to whom a missive was addressed, and even reading all of the postal cards.

When he finished he mounted his bronco and rode away. Neither Pony nor the stranger knew whether he had found anything for himself or whether he had taken any mail with him. It was customary for whoever got there first to take the mail to everyone who lived along his route when he started for home, without saying anything about it.

Pony, of course, knew that.

By this time the stranger probably suspected it.

Pony said afterwards he could see the man swelling little by little until he looked like he "was agoin' tuh bust."

Pony must have been doing a little swelling himself, judging from the conversation which followed.

"I am a United States postal inspector," said the stranger, trembling with rage, "and I want to know if that is the way you conduct the business of this United States postoffice."

Pony stared at him in silence. Then he arose, also in silence. The stranger arose also.

Pony, without a word, lifted the "United States postoffice" from its resting place on the shelf, and walked to the creek a few yards from the door.

"That," he said, "is the way I conduct the business of this United States postoffice, you and the United States postoffice can both go to h *h*."

With that he dropped the can, caught it on the toe of his boot and kicked it across the creek, scattering its contents far and wide.

And that is why the postoffice called Pony, Montana, is now in Madison county, instead of in Fergus county, for that was the end of Pony McPhartland's postoffice.[1]

Madison County's Pony was founded by Tecumseh Smith, called "Pony" because he was such a "little runt."

Pony, who had staked out a claim earlier, came back to the gulch—that was to be named after him—with a partner in 1868. In 1875 a miner swung a pick through some wild strawberry plants and discovered a vein called the Strawberry.

As the stamp mills sprang up and began their noisy operation, Pony Smith's feet began to itch for quieter, perhaps richer, camps. He left, and before long the cost-profit squeeze took its toll and the mines closed down.

Today, remains of the Elling and Morris mill perch above Pony, while below, the 100 or so residents try to keep their town from dying completely. Sandwiched between the mines and the active part of town are the meat market and empty stores. Of interest is the Morris State Bank, which until recently served as the Mines Sales Leasing Agency of the district. It's a well-preserved structure with picturesque teller's cages, colonnaded stone entrance, and lettering still clinging to unbroken windows.

Only time will dictate whether the second town will perish along with the first named Pony.

Many of the tales heard in Pony evolve around Marshal William B. Landon, rock-chiseller par excellence.

One of the marshal's enduring works can be found near the town of Potosi, where he scrawled, "One Mile to Hell."

Near the city dump is another Landon masterpiece consisting of strange letters, Landon's initials, a maltese cross, and the date of 1921. Rumor has it around Pony that the marshal did it all as a joke, thinking some of the more gullible would think it was a secret treasure map.

Marshal Landon even carved his own tombstone.

Near Pony is Red Bluff, which prior to 1864 was a stage stop. In 1864 a two-story stone miner's boardinghouse was built and used until the turn of the century, at which time it was converted into a residence. Later it was used as a hotel, and currently is home of the Red Bluff Research Station of Montana State University.

The research station, a cemetery, a mine tunnel, and a few cabins mark what was once a town of perhaps 1,000.

Two indispensable tools in assaying: a bone ash cupel, left, and a crucible

1. Originally printed in the *Hardin Tribune Herald*, February 13, 1937. Mail delivery problems occurred not only at post offices. Mail would often lie in a given place for months awaiting pick-up. Often first-class mail was in sacks with a copper padlock; second-class with an iron padlock; and third-class was secured with a puckering string.

RADERSBURG: How Brother Van closed the saloon.

Last-day-of-school picnics were often held in the back yard of the IOOF hall in Radersburg

Toston, where there is supposed to be a small blast furnace to treat ores from Radersburg

The first lump of free-milling gold ore was found in the Radersburg area in the early 1860s. It wasn't until John A. Keating began working his mine in 1866 that Radersburg attracted much attention from miners.

Later, placer gold was discovered, which meant water was necessary—a scarce commodity in the area. William Quinn and his company dug a five-mile ditch to bring the precious water to the operations. Another ditch supplied the Gulches—Faith, Hope, and Charity. Joe Poe hauled water from Crow Creek to Radersburg during the winter months. Supplies were also scarce. The nearest railroad point was Corinne, Utah, about 500 miles distant, and prices were high. Radersburg residents had to pay twenty-five cents for an apple and a dollar for a pound of flour to compensate freighters, who made the trip in four to six months.

In 1879 the population of Radersburg was 250. The following year it was 69. It's managed to hold its own, with latest population figures estimated at 80.

The old Odd Fellows Hall has an interesting history. It was built by a man named Johnson to function as a carpenter shop; living quarters were on the second story. Mr. Johnson was the father of Mrs. Della Williams, who was the mother of movie actress Myrna Loy.

Radersburg became the county seat of Jefferson County when the county was organized in 1869.

The Radersburg jail was moved down the street and used as a saloon until prohibition. Periodically it has been used as a restaurant or bakery

A combined courthouse-jail was built on a hill in the middle of town at a cost of $26,000. As Radersburg lost population, the county seat was moved to Boulder, in 1886. The courthouse was used as a schoolhouse until 1912, thereafter as a meeting hall and polling place. In about 1920 the structure was sold, and a barn was built from it. The barn still stands on a farm north of town.

The jail was moved down to the main street and used as a saloon until Prohibition. Later, the jail was used as a restaurant and bakery. It was run by a lady with a very conspicuous wax nose. Whether she had her nose cut off when someone threw a beer bottle when she was tending bar years before, or whether she was in a fight and had the nose bitten off remains a point of speculation in Radersburg.[1]

One of Radersburg's characters boasted he had not had a bath since his mother last gave him one. Tales persist that when he picked up his mail-order bride in Butte, she wasn't too impressed, but married him anyway, since she was lacking funds to return East. But she wouldn't live with him. The story goes that when he called on his wife, she would set a chair by the door, place newspapers on the chair and floor, and chat with him—at a distance.[2]

The Methodist circuit rider, Brother Van (W. W. Van Orsdale), frequently held services in Radersburg. One local businessman had no love for the popular preacher. One hot summer day when Brother Van was preaching, he left his horse tied up for several hours. The merchant had Brother Van arrested on a charge of cruelty to animals. Brother Van acted in his own defense and won the ensuing trial. The presiding judge requested that the preacher suggest an appropriate sentence. Although the prosecutor isn't usually "sentenced" when the defendant is acquitted, so went Montana justice. The penalty was leveled: attend church once a month for the rest of your life. And so it was, even after Brother Van's death, the merchant dutifully donned his "Sunday-go-to-meetin' " clothes whenever services were held, which was about once a month.

It was Brother Van, indirectly, who was responsible for Radersburg's "near-miracle." A few years after Van Orsdale's death, the district superintendent of the Methodist church came to Radersburg to hold services and talk about Brother Van. An eyewitness says, "Hardly any men ever attended church there under most circumstances, but on that occasion the pool hall[3] closed for the first time in its existence."[4]

1. Personal letter, Mrs. William Guntermann, April 20, 1970.
2. *Ibid.*
3. For all intents and purposes, the saloon.
4. Guntermann letter.

RIMINI:

Where a case of dysentery saved a life.

A typical structure at Rimini

An older section of Rimini

Though all are not architectural masterpieces, many structures of interest can be found in Rimini

Rimini, Montana may have been named after a city on the east coast of Italy or for the drama *Francesca Da Rimini*, which was performed by a traveling troupe there during its formative years. No matter how inaccessible the history of the origin of the town, Rimini (pronounced RIM-in-eye) is a physically accessible ghost town because the road leading to it was built on an old railroad right-of-way. Originally the town was named Young Ireland.

During the winter Rimini is almost a ghost town, but several cabins, many modified from half-century-old structures, are occupied during the summer.

People in Rimini, as in many places, are not adverse to "borrowing" parts of deserted structures to help improve their domiciles.

The modifications give a crazy patchwork atmosphere to the town—the main street lined with abandoned structures, and occasionally a well-preserved vintage cabin, or another structure part old, part new.

The rich mountainsides surrounding Rimini on the east slope of the Continental Divide have been extensively worked.

It's said that one night the dam above the town broke and tons of water came crashing down, miraculously bowling over only one cabin. The owner was fortunate in that he suffered the lesser of two evils. He had dysentery and was in the outhouse at the time the waters came tumbling down. He lived.

An old log cabin remodelled several times

Rimini's new Main Street

A typical combination of new and old

A false-fronted log building at Rimini

Log, siding and cinder block construction at Rimini

ROCHESTER:

Once a two-woman town.

The ghost town of Rochester was born near Twin Bridges in the 1860s. By 1869 about 800 men existed in the dry sagebrush-choked, sheep-grazing country. Although there wasn't enough water to support placer mining arrastres were used for a brief time, supplanted by stamp mills. But partly because of a lack of water, even the most efficient mills lost nearly fifty percent of the gold run through them.[1]

The Watseca mines were the most productive, but they and the few others in the area were almost exhausted in less than ten years from their beginnings.

There was a revival of Rochester in the early 1870s that continued through the early 1900s, when the town's population ballooned to about 5,000. Then the population dwindled until 1926, when a short recovery began. After 1932, Rochester slowly died.

Two sisters stayed for twenty years in the decaying ruins of Rochester. The widows, Mrs. Lucy Miller and Etta Fisher, lived a quarter of a mile apart. They faced many hardships. The wells went dry, so in season they canned water from melted snow. When they could no longer gather firewood, they bought fuel and water from the nearest town, thirteen miles away, along a tortuous, unimproved road. Neither drove a car, so their contacts with civilization were few. For weeks at a time they were completely isolated until the mailman would come or friends would drop into see how they were doing.

When the sisters could no longer cope with the rugged existence in Rochester, one went to live with relatives, the other to a rest home.[2] Their cabins, plus a few other structures, including the imposing Hardesty Hotel, succumbed shortly after their departure.

Hunters in the Rochester area have torn buildings apart for firewood. The landmark hotel was sold by the county for back taxes for around $22. The purchaser reportedly sold the lumber for a profit of about ten times his original investment. Vandals and nearby ranchers have taken most of what else remained of this town which once boasted a population of about 5,000.

Greasewood, sagebrush and cactus reclaim the townsite of Rochester

Today, a few head of sheep graze the area. Seepage from the deserted mines has caused a contemporary pollution problem. Water from the copper-rich mines has flowed into nearby gullies and gulches. A sheep rancher whose flocks graze nearby was thankful to learn, when he sent a water sample to the state laboratory, that the water from one of the old mines was safe to drink—for sheep.

All that remains of Rochester is a few rock and stone foundations plus a fenced-in graveyard, which is somehow free of the cactus, greasewood, and sagebrush that choke the area that once was the town.

Arid conditions around Rochester made placer mining difficult

The grave stone of these triplets reflects the hard life of the frontier

1. Wolle, *Montana Pay Dirt*, p. 207.
2. That was in 1952, when Mrs. Lucy Miller was eighty years old and Mrs. Etta Fisher seventy-five, according to the *Montana Standard-Butte Daily Post*, June 14, 1964.

SUNRISE | When the alarm clock rings, what ghosts arise?

After a long hibernation, this bed, left in Sunrise, Montana's only cabin, was appropriated by an antique fancier, more than 100 years after the beginning of Montana's gold rush

A person can go from Sunrise to Sunset in about two hours. The former is a mining camp near Hall, Montana; the latter an old lumber camp overlooking the Blackfoot River not far from Coloma.

Sunrise was born with the Waseca claim, the first patented mine in Montana. But it was deserted in the silver panic near the turn of the century.

Almost a half century later, it was reopened with the hope that it could again produce silver through large-scale dredging.

When the second wave of miners came, they found engineers' charts and even the dinner bell still hanging outside the mess hall door. They also found a marker warning that six Chinamen were buried in the area.

But they didn't find silver which could be economically mined.

Today, little remains of Sunrise, Montana. One cabin stood until recently with a gold-painted metal bed with headboard and footboard intact.

On the "outskirts" of Sunrise, a mill and sundry structures slowly decay.

Clearly with each dying sunset, Sunrise's date with extinction moves one day closer.

Twice-born, twice-dead: Sunrise, Montana

The rapidly deteriorating remains of mining activity at Sunrise

THE SUPERIOR AREA:

Where miners still toil.

An ore train parked on the shute above the Iron Mountain Mill, 1896
—Courtesy, Bill Pike

West of Missoula, near Superior, are many ghost town sites in varying states of decay. There are Mayville, Martina City, Forest City, Louisville, Cayuse, Amador, Quartz, Perma, Paradise, Saltese, Taft, Silver City, Cedar Creek, Jamestown, Mugginsville, Moose Creek, Pardee, and Keystone (known earlier as Carter). Most have disappeared, some are inhabited, two are true ghosts. Population counts are not available, but the *Weekly Missoulian* reported the population of Louisville on Sept. 2, 1874, as being three souls and a ghost.

Not all the buildings in Keystone have fallen, and not all are extremely old. The general store now has found a new lease on life—hay is stored in it. Most of the remaining sod-roofed cabins are small.

At Pardee, a few shacks remain, as well as remnants of a mill. Tracks used for transporting silver ore from the Iron Mountain mine are still there. But little else remains of a city which once rivaled Beartown and Butte as the roughest in the state.

In the area are several operating placer and hardrock mines.

For an interesting side trip, there's the Gildersleeve mine, about two dozen miles south of Superior.

Here, George and Fern Gildersleeve work both placer and underground mines, and welcome guests to their charming home and fairly extensive mining operations. They can even put up visitors for the night in rustic accommodations formerly inhabited by mine workers.

Fern is a cook in the Superior school system during non-mining months and makes attractive jewelry using gold she and her husband have mined.

In addition to drilling cores, foundations and a flume, the mill, a tramway and ore buckets remain at the Gold Mountain Mine along Deep Creek, south of Superior

Amador about 1905. In the foreground is the train which ran along Cedar Creek. The building on the left was Masser's Saloon. On the right is the office building of the McCabe and Amador Mining Company
—Courtesy, Bill Pike

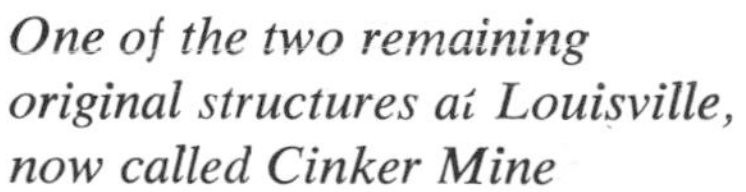

One of the two remaining original structures at Louisville, now called Cinker Mine

A ghostly remnant of Amador. Gold was first discovered at the Amador Mine site in 1872, but area was not extensively worked until about 1900

The warmth of the hearth fire in Ado Koehmstadt's cabin was sufficient to entice a visit by a bear

Ado vows if there's gold, "I'll find it"

The exterior of a typical miner's cabin; this one belonging to Ado Koehmstadt in Montana's Windfall Country

Ado dams up the water in a pond until there's enough pressure built up to trip the flood gate and send the water cascading down the stream to expose new earth and hopefully, new gold-bearing deposits

Ado "booming." Through the "booming" process, materials are moved in the creek bed to expose the gold bearing areas

One of George's avocational talents is making excellent home brew—an especially refreshing concoction made from cool, sparkling, pure mountain water.

The Gildersleeve mine is one of the few places where a still-operational "hydraulic giant" can be found.

The mining claims have been in the family for years.

Nearby are hardrock mining operations.

Visitors to the mine don miners' lamps and enter mine shafts, hear the whir of ventilation and water pumping systems, and see dynamite blasting operations, drifting methods, and ore specimens. They can listen to the philosophies and histories of the miners—of claim jumping, of the pressures of the larger mining operations against the small independent operators. The hours pass quickly in the company of these independent holdovers from a colorful era.

On the sad side of the ledger, here, too, can be heard the hack of "rocks in the box"; or "miner's con," silicosis, the dreaded miners' disease. Finitely small, but highly abrasive, dust from the mines enters the miners' lungs and frequently causes fatal respiratory problems.

Within a few miles, in the Windfall country, are such interesting operations as that of Ado Koehmstadt.

Ado, a retired sheet metal worker bothered by emphysema, built a highly sophisticated fireplace in his cabin, as well as an efficient refrigeration system and a power generator, and he has designed a most unusual system of ponds, flood gates, counterweights, and mining machinery to scratch out a living as a fair-weather miner.

Ado has had his troubles with cantankerous bears; one even had the discourtesy to fall through his cabin roof.

A Chinese bathhouse squats on Ado's property. The Chinese often came to supposedly worked-out diggings and somehow managed to wash out thousands of dollars worth of dust and nuggets after every one else had gone on to more "profitable" operations. So while many Chinese washed clothes, many others washed gravel. Often they would pan the wash water to pick up gold lodged in miners' clothing. They had been known to rip up wooden floors of saloons to get the gold which had sifted through the cracks in the floor.[1]

At nearby Cayuse, the Chinese Cayuse Flume Company is believed to have washed out millions of dollars worth of gold after the Irish miners moved on.

In many stream beds around Superior and elsewhere, "colors" still can be found and the modern visitor can pan out a few dollars worth of gold. But the water is cold and the dust niggardly.

Accounts of miners' frustrations about the Government's rare mineral policies and the pressures exerted by large mining interests are frequently voiced

A hydraulic giant in operation. Dammed-up streams of water are directed against stream beds to dislodge gold-bearing areas making them more accessible to the gold pan

Long time mine owner, George Gildersleeve pans for gold at one of his placer operations

Above these burned-out ruins of the mill at Pardee is the Iron Mountain Mine, one of the state's best silver producers between 1888 and 1896

Hauling cordwood near Pardee —Courtesy, Bill Pike

A pair of ore buckets south of Superior

The best cabin remaining in Keystone

The only intact building remaining in Pardee

The Keystone General Merchandise Emporium

Miners at Pardee about 1896—Courtesy, Bill Pike

Mine workers probably lived in these buildings on Pardee's main street

Joe Gareau's Saloon at Iron Mountain, 1912 —Courtesy, Bill Pike

An Interior view of Gareau's Saloon, 1912 —Courtesy, Bill Pike

Keystone about 1900 —Courtesy, Bill Pike

Iron Mountain about 1896—Courtesy, Bill Pike

1. The Chinese were not the only ones who did such. A man bought a saloon in Virginia City, had it torn down; using a rocker, he reclaimed $10,000 worth of dust that had sifted through the floor boards.

Remains of the Quartz Hill Mine, enroute to Vipond

VIPOND:

Where nature has reclaimed her domain.

One of three structures remaining in Vipond

In 1868 John Vipond discovered the first lode in the Quartz Canyon Creek mining district. He named the mine the Mewonitoc. The following year, he and two brothers, plus other prospectors, developed the area in what is known as Vipond Park, and at nearby Quartz Hill. There was no way to get the ores out of the area, north of Dillon, so the miners built roads to get mule teams to Corinne, Utah. The ore was then shipped to Swansea, Wales, for refining.

One of the more successful operations, the Lone Pine, was sold in 1891 to an English syndicate for $725,000. The Jay Hawk Mining Company was well-managed and invested $50,000 in the operation. The stamp mill at Dewey was moved to the area, and ten stamps were added to the original fifteen. A concentrating plant was added. The mines were doing well, producing about $33,000 in silver each month. The firm was said by many to be one of the best-managed in the West. Still, the drop in the price of silver forced the company to close its operations in 1895.

Since then, some mining has gone on in the area on an irregular basis.

Today, three structures remain, and timber wolves and whitetail deer inhabit the nearby meadows. Half a dozen miles away, the Quartz Hill operations continue.

VIRGINIA CITY, BANNACK, ET AL:

Where the biggest and richest gold strikes were.

The areas of Alder Gulch and Grasshopper Creek in southeastern Montana were the sites of Montana's richest gold discoveries. On July 28, 1862, John White discovered gold on Grasshopper Creek. Bannack grew up on the site. A more spectacular strike occurred the following year, 1863. Five prospectors led by Bill Fairweather were on their way to the Yellowstone country in search of diggin's. Unfortunately, a band of Crows stood between them and their destination and they were captured.

Accounts of how they escaped vary.[1] In one story it's said Bill Fairweather grabbed a snake and, by that brave act, impressed the Indians so much the prospectors were set free.

In the second tale, Fairweather is reported to have grabbed a sacred medicine bush and hit the medicine man with it. While the braves opted for the white man's scalp, Chief Red Bear orated for ten hours in defense of Fairweather and crew. The warriors gave in to their chief's wishes rather than listen to his palaver any longer, and the white men were set free.

The third story has a friendly squaw going to the gang at night and leading them to safety.

The truth would seem to be otherwise. Party member Henry Edgar kept a diary, and a man who was sufficiently meticulous about detail to note that on the evening of May 26th the party ate venison and the next day elk probably would remember what happened during the life-and-death encounter earlier that same month.

He recounts: "I don't know how it was, but a rattlesnake would never bite Bill [Fairweather]. When he saw one he would always grab it up and carry it along with him a ways. They never seemed to resent anything he would do to them and he never killed one. As we were going toward this Indian village he picked up a rattlesnake and just at the outskirts of the village he picked up another. When the Indians saw him come in with a rattlesnake on each arm they were awed. He put the snakes in his shirt bosom and Simmons [Lewis Simmons] told the Indians he was the great medicine man of the whites."[2]

Virginia City, 1866—Courtesy, Montana Historical Society

Virginia City—Courtesy Montana Historical Society

Virginia City's Company "D" of the Montana Militia in front of the courthouse
—Courtesy, Montana Historical Society

Edgar also had some recollections about the medicine bush incident: "They took us into the medicine lodge, where there was a big bush in the center. They marched us around that bush several times and finally Bill said if they marched him around again he would pull up the sacred medicine bush. They marched us around again and Bill pulled up the bush and walloped the medicine man on the head with it. We then formed three to three, back to back. We had refused all along to give up our guns and revolvers. The old chief drove the other Indians back with a whip. They had a council which lasted from noon until midnight. In the morning we got our sentence. If we went on they would kill us. If we went back and would give up our horses we would not be harmed. It was Hobson's choice."[3]

According to Edgar's account, the men were worse off when they left the Crow camp than when they arrived. He doesn't indicate how the other members of the party fared, but of himself recounts: "I got for my three horses an old horse, blind in one eye, and a yearling colt. For my three pairs of Oregon blankets I got a buffalo robe and a half, and for my grub, consisting of flour, bacon, coffee, beans, etc., I got a dozen dried buffalo tongues."[4]

The version of the encounter relating to the squaw could have been based on what Edgar says happened the next day. "We met an old squaw woman, who warned us not to cross the river, and we didn't. Instead, we took up into the mountains and camped there until morning, fearful of the Indians. In the morning we saw thirty or forty of them looking at our trail. We camped until night and then crossed to the south side of the river. . . . We found the Indians were ahead of us and had taken over the hills . . . we came on over the pass . . . and saw the Indians coming up the valley. We concealed ourselves in the brush along the creek and exchanged shots with them. There was a parley. They agreed that if we came out they would not harm us, but we wouldn't trust them. We waited until dark and then struck out. . . ."[5]

Later that day, May 26, 1863, after they made camp, Fairweather noticed some rimrock which looked rich in gold. It was. There were scads.[6] The next day the six panned out $180 in gold.[7]

On May 30th, after panning more gold and staking their claims, the group left Alder Gulch (so named by Edgar for the alder trees lining the gulch)[8] and went the dozen miles to Bannack to replenish supplies.

After whooping it up in Bannack's rowdyhouses, the group left on June 2nd, heading back for

Originally, the graves of 13 road agents lined Virginia City's Boot Hill. Now there are 5

An outing of the Virginia City Rifle Team—Courtesy Montana Historical Society

Putting up their "dukes" in a display of pugilistic prowess in a Virginia City saloon — Courtesy, Montana Historical Society

Wm. W. Morris came to Virginia City in June, 1864. He opened a drug store in the building shown, where 5 road agents were hanged from a beam—Courtesy, Montana Historical Society

Robber's Roost originally designed as a roadhouse between Virginia City and Bannack, became a haven for robbers. Drinkers and gamblers frequented the first floor. The second floor was a dance hall. Bullet holes in the walls would indicate that an occasional stand-off for the attention of a fickle siren was settled in true western tradition

their finds. But they were not alone; about 200 followed them, hungry for a share of the gold.

The Fairweather party tried to shake the followers from their trail, but finally realized this couldn't be done. On June 4th they proposed that if the others promised not to jump the Fairweather group's claims, they could share the rest of the riches of the gulch and twelve-mile-long Alder Creek.[9] And there was plenty of wealth to share. The first year 1,000 men averaged $10,000 each from the rich diggin's.[10]

In the summer of 1864, Colonel Daniel H. Hunkins built what was perhaps the state's first steam-operated quartz mill. Hunkins had the machinery hauled to Fort Saint Charles on the Missouri River then to Bannack.[11] The mill was probably in nearby Centerville (Marysville). Nearby was another small settlement—Jerusalem.

Soon a town was born near the bonanza. It was named Varina, in honor of the wife of Jefferson Davis. District Judge G. G. Bissel took violent exception to the name; his sentiments were clearly anti-Confederate. The good magistrate refused to enter the name in his court records, and substituted "Virginia City" as the official name of the settlement. Neither Confederate nor Union sympathizers objected to the new monicker. Other shebangs[12] spawned in and near the gulch were Nevada City, Adobetown, Ruby, Alder, Laurin, Junction City, Central, Highland, Pine Grove, and Summit. All were influenced by the town on Grasshopper Creek, territorial capital Bannack.

Incorporated in January, 1864, Virginia City prospered and took the honor of being territorial capital away from Bannack the next year. Virginia City inherited something else from Bannack—the murdering, gambling, woman-chasing road agent par excellence Henry Plummer.

Claim jumping, thievery by bartenders who used extra-long fingernails to gather in just a smidgen more gold dust from pokes than was fair, "high-grading" (stealing high-grade ore), and crimes of passion were common in this raw land. But the Plummer era of lawlessness was unique. More than 100 travelers were murdered and uncounted hoards of gold taken by the Plummer gang (which may have numbered between 75 and 100),[13] mostly in the seventy-mile stretch between Bannack and Virignia City:

Born of "gentle upbringing" in Connecticut and coming to Montana *via* Nevada, California, and Idaho, Henry Plummer reached Bannack in March, 1862.

Young, handsome, well-liked, a leader of men and follower of women, Plummer was elected sheriff of Bannack.[14] But for Henry Plummer, this wasn't

An overview of Bannack during the gold rush —Courtesy, Montana Historical Society

enough—Bannack was at one end of the well-traveled avenues for hauling gold. Virginia City was at the other. So Plummer forced the sheriff of Virginia City to vacate that office and happily took it over himself.

The facade began to wear thin shortly after he married Eliza (or Electa) Bryan. Plummer was frequently seen with some of the town's more undesirable characters; among them were a horsethief, a gunman, road agents and a suspected cannibal.

Plummer's "innocents," as they called themselves, headquartered at the Rattlesnake Ranch east of Bannack, and often met at Robber's Roost, also known as Pete Daly's Place,[15] twelve miles from Virginia City. Plummer, leaving town on some pretense, often rode with his road agents. Among them were Whiskey Bill Graves, George Ives, Boone Helm, Ned Ray, Buck Stinson, George Shears, Red Yeager, Cyrus Skinner, and perhaps Mexican Frank. At times Plummer stayed at his office, acting much surprised when he was told of the robberies.[16]

It's not clear just when the citizens of Bannack, Virginia City, Nevada City, and the other camps in the area began to have some misgivings about the integrity of the lawman. "Bummer Dan" was probably one of the first to uncover the truth.

Through a fluke, "Bummer" managed to make a modest strike of several thousand dollars in gold and decided to go back East to enjoy himself.[17]

However, the Innocents were aware of Bummer Dan's intentions and held up the stage between Alder Gulch and Bannack. They netted $7,000, although the unhappy miner-about-to-become-gentle-

BATHS
TOBACCO AND

Gallows at Bannack

Like Virginia City, many structures in neighboring Nevada City have been restored, rebuilt, or moved in from other sites, to show visitors what a western mining town might have looked like

man managed to hide one sack of gold from the two holdup men.

Bummer Dan gave Sheriff Plummer "what for" for allowing such lawless acts. The sheriff must have been impressed. He's reported to have said, "Never mind: when I get my cut, I'll return your money."[18]

Though no mental giant, Bummer Dan understood what that slip of the tongue meant. He vamoosed!

A boy who worked for Chief Justice Sidney Edgerton (Edgerton later became territorial governor) told Edgerton he knew what Sheriff Plummer was doing—young Henry Tilden was held up by masked men and when one of the agents' masks slipped, Tilden recognized the sheriff.

It was also reported that during one holdup Plummer was recognized not by his face, but by his hands.

In the meantime, aroused citizens in the camps in the area had decided the authorities couldn't or wouldn't enforce the law and had begun planning to mete out their own brand of justice.

Perhaps the murder of Nicholas Thiebalt (or Tiebalt)[19] for a total take of $200 tipped the balance. When the suspected killers of Thiebalt (Long John Franck, George Hilderman, and George Ives) were rounded up on a cold December day in 1863, citizen justice began to roll in Nevada City. Seeing what might happen, one of the Innocents, "Club Foot" George Lane, rode to Bannack to tell Sheriff Plummer of the doings. Plummer wisely stayed away from the scene.

After a trial running from one afternoon to the next, a twenty-four man jury decided that Ives was guilty of the murder of Thiebalt. Ives was hanged, the other two banished.[20]

Hundreds in the area insisted this was only the beginning. Five men in Virginia City, one in Nevada City, and several from Bannack began to organize a vigilance committee. These men were the vanguard of the famed Montana Vigilantes.

The vigilance committee was headed by the effective John Xavier ("X") Beidler.

They used the sign: 3-7-77. When the symbol appeared on a suspect's door, he left town. The tale most commonly accepted today is that the sign stood for the dimensions of a grave: three feet wide, seven feet long and seventy-seven inches deep. Some say the symbol meant that a man had three hours, seven minutes and seventy-seven seconds to skedaddle. Others say each member of the vigilance committee had an identifying code number, and Vigilantes 3, 7, and 77 once signed a warning that way.[21] Many were warned, but most road agents were not. Some were hanged, some banished, some lashed with a bull whip.

There is controversy over the wording of the Vigilante oath. One version is this:

> We the undersigned united oursel in a party for the laudible purpos of arresting thievs & murders & recove stollen property do pledge ourselves upon our sacred honor each to all others & solumnly swear that we will reveal no secrets violate no laws of right & not desert each other or our standard of justice so help us God as with our hand & seal this 23 of December A.D. 1863.[22]

Members of the secret organization combed the mountains and valleys and bars and gulches and gullies and wikiups[23] and cabins for their prey.

Just before Red Yeager was hanged, he named Henry Plummer as the leader of the road agents. In January, Plummer and deputies Buck Stinson and Ned Ray were brought to trial and found guilty. Plummer offered his weight in gold to be set free—but there were no takers. A gallows Plummer had ordered built for a prisoner was the one used for the sheriff and his two deputies. That was on January 10th. On the 13th, the search for six of Plummer's gang was begun. One escaped, five were captured. The Vigilantes decided to hang all five simultaneously from a roof beam of an unfinished house. When the nooses had been placed, the men were ordered to step up on boxes. Ropes were snugged around the necks of Frank Parrish, Club Foot George (George Lane),[24] Boone Helm, Jack Gallagher,[25] and Haze Lyon and the boxes kicked out from under them. After the bodies were cut down, they were laid in front of various buildings in Virginia City. The grave markers of the five road agents are still on a hill overlooking town.

Thirteen of Plummer's gang were strung up and buried on the hill between December 20, 1863, and February 5, 1864. Twenty-two felons, including Plummer, were hanged. The grave sites of all are not known, and not all were buried with great ceremony. Plummer's body was thrown into a pit which already contained the remains of George Ives. A pile of stone marked the spot in Hangman's Gulch.

Then, through the efforts of Dr. John Glick of Bannack, Plummer's remains were partially exhumed. The physician had treated the sheriff, at gunpoint, for a bullet wound. The doctor's curiosity got the better of him; he wanted to see if the bullet he thought remained in Plummer's right forearm was still there. Taking leave of the dance he was attending, Dr. Glick severed the arm, stored it in a snow drift and returned to the soirée. A dog found the arm and dragged it to his mistress, who was attending the dance. Dr. Glick kept his cool, retrieved the arm, and managed to examine it later. He found the bullet.[26]

A Wells, Fargo & Company stage at Virginia City

The bones of Henry Plummer still weren't destined to rest. Two drunks in Bannack opened the grave and stole Plummer's skull. The skull rested in relative peace in the Bank Exchange saloon for a number of years.[27] It's not known where Plummer's remains are now.

Although sometimes ruthless, the Vigilantes were usually efficient. Once they got out of hand. Joe Pizanthia, "The Greaser," was hiding in his cabin. Seeing two pursuing Vigilantes approaching, he shot at both, killing one and wounding the other. The crowd shouted for vengeance. But they felt the life of The Greaser was not worth risking yet another life. Ultimately the group decided their strategy. It happened there was a mountain howitzer available. They blasted away at The Greaser's cabin three times. Thinking they had wounded or killed their quarry, they advanced. Smith Ball, whom the Mexican had wounded during the initial attack, found Pizanthia and emptied his revolver into the man, and the suspect was made ready for the next step—hanging. Nathaniel P. Langford, a member of the Vigilante executive committee, describes the scene: "A clothes-line near was taken down, and fastened round his neck, and an ambitious citizen climbed a pole, and, while those below held up the body of the expiring Mexican, he fastened the rope to the top of the pole. Into the body thus suspended, the crowd discharged more than a hundred shots—satiating their thirst for revenge upon a ghostly corpse."[28]

Finally, the body of The Greaser was hurled onto a huge pyre made from wood from his cabin. The story goes that the cremation was so complete nothing remained, not even gold dust, which several "soiled doves"[29] tried to pan from the ashes the next morning.

The vigilance committees were formed out of necessity, and almost without exception fairly performed their tasks. In one exception, James Daniels had been sentenced to prison for murder. General Meagher, secretary of the Montana Territory, pardoned him. The Vigilantes got Daniels and hanged him anyway, pinning a message to Meagher on the decedent's coat advising Meagher if he pardoned another prisoner, he'd be hanged.

The Vigilantes were feared by many. On March 2, 1867, three years and one month after the Vigilantes hanged their last victim, the Montana *Post* indicated the residents of nearby Red Mountain

Bon Accord Dredge, reconstructed—Courtesy, Sassman

City posted a notice in which they ". . . solemnly swear that the first man that is hung by the Vigilantes of this place we will retaliate five for one. . . . You must not think you can do as you please. We are American citizens, and you shall not drive and hang whom you please."

The vigilance committees usually got their man, but on a few occasions didn't "launch them into eternity" with absolute efficiency or humanity. Dimsdale, who was there, cites instances.

Of the hanging of George Shears he writes: "The drop was long and the rope tender. It slowly untwisted, and Shears hung, finally, by a single strand. George's parting question was, for a long time, a by-word among the Vigilantes."

Henry Plummer, Ned Ray, and Buck Stinson were to be strung up at the same time. Of Plummer's death, Dimsdale says, "He died quickly and without much struggle."

Of Stinson, Dimsdale writes. "By a sudden twist of his head at the moment of his elevation, the knot slipped under his chin, and he was some minutes dying."

Ray's execution was even less efficient, "Being loosely pinioned, he got his fingers between the rope and his neck, and thus prolonged his misery. . . . It was necessary to seize Ned Ray's hand, and by a violent effort to draw his fingers from between the noose and his neck before he died. Probably he was the last to expire of the guilty trio." He was the first of the three to be strung up.

Once the Vigilantes took action against one of their own. Joseph A. (Jack) Slade was a reckless man who had done more than his share of killing. He was likeable when sober, but a mean varmint when imbibing. The citizens didn't mind Slade's charging down the streets, yelling and shooting his six-shooter, but they were very upset when Slade rode his horse through stores and bars.

A people's court had been set up with judge and jury to partially replace the swift and not always impartial justice of the Vigilante committee.

Slade had appeared before the court on more occasions than one, always sober and apologetic. But on one March morning, after the warrant charging Slade with disorderly conduct was read, Slade yanked it from Sheriff Fox and tore it up and crushed it with his heel. Slade drew his derringer and threatened presiding Judge Davis with it.

The grave markers of three of Henry Plummer's gang—Ned Ray, Joe Pizanthia and Buck Stinson—are at the foot of a reconstructed gallows

Plummer's headquarters were at Rattlesnake Ranch; but the gang also met at Dempsey's Cottonwood Ranch, Daley's "Robber's Roost" at Ramshorn Gulch, and ranches and wikiups on the Madison and Jefferson Rivers, Wisconsin Creek and Mill Creek

3-7-77.
ROBBER'S ROOST.
3-7-77-

The Virginia City band and orchestra members—Courtesy, Montana Historical Society

Then, remnants of the Vigilante committee, who had met previously and decided Slade must be liquidated, grabbed the still-drunk prisoner and hanged him from a corral gate.

Virginia (Molly) Slade had been told of the trouble her husband was in, but arrived on the scene too late.[30] Slade's body had already been cut down and was reposing in the Virginia Hotel.

Three months later she left by coach for Salt Lake City accompanying Slade's body, which was in a metal coffin filled with alcohol.[31]

Today Virginia City is a popular place, along with its sister city a mile away, Nevada City; not so much for ghost town buffs, but more for those who would like to see what a western mining town really looked like. Some structures have been preserved, some reproduced, some moved in from elsewhere.

An old stone barn is now a theatre. The old Gilbert Brewery, the Bale O' Hay Saloon, and many other structures, including that housing Montana's first newspaper, *The Montana Post*, are popular attractions in Virginia City; but there are many in Nevada City and Bannack, too.

To give some idea of the journalistic tone of that time, the following is reprinted from the *Montana Democrat*, a competitor of the *Montana Post*:

> Last night between the hours of 9 and 10 o'clock, J. D. Judd, alias Essner, alias Weston . . . made his escape. Furnished by some one with a file and saw, he succeeded in removing the shackles from his legs, removed the iron bars over the door of his cell and reached the outer apartment of the prison. He then sawed one of the logs apart, that composed the ceiling of the jail, and reached the attick from which, by removing some planks, he descended into the cooking room in the front part of the building. He had a large bowie knife and induced the other prisoners . . . to keep quiet. . . . He had prepared about 20 pounds of flour to take with him. . . . He was discovered, and . . . immediately escaped through a front window, but was forced to drop the flour. . . . He left a note behind him of a malicious character, evidentally designed to reflect upon parties who were conspicious in his arrest. . . . Upon the back of it was the following endorsement: "Departure of Judd & Co. per lightning express. February 20th, 1868."

Between Bannack and Virginia City, "Robber's Roost" still stands—the hangout for Plummer's gang; the place they appropriated from the owner by hanging him from his own door post.

The first church established in 1877 by "Brother Van" (William Van Orsdell), the famous Methodist Circuit Rider

The first electric gold dredge was launched May 15, 1895. The remains of the G. L. Graves electric dredge boat now rests in Grasshopper Creek

Interior of Virginia City Mercantile

Northwest of Virginia City is Ruby, scene of extensive dredging operations.

Perhaps the most fascinating part of Ruby's history concerns these operations. The first gold dredge was the Maggie A. Gibson, supplanted by a succession of progressively larger "gold boats."

Six dredge boats operated in Beaverhead County. The Fielding L. Graves was reported to be the first successful gold dredge in the United States. It was launched on Grasshopper Creek May 15, 1895. The "Maggie A. Gibson" was originally launched on Grasshopper Creek on May 23, 1897, and later taken to Alder Gulch. The Bannack Dredging Company launched the "Graeter" dredge on July 12, 1897. During the autumn of 1897 an English corporation, the Bon Accord Company, launched a dredge. The last to be launched was the "Coast" dredge, on Grasshopper Creek, which was later taken to Oregon. The "Brenner" was launched in 1899. Draglines have been operated on Grasshopper Creek as late as 1939.[32]

Norman Weis recounts a highlight of the era of dredging operations near Ruby:

"Electric power was available in 1906, and new plans were drawn for a mammoth 'all electrical' machine. It was to be larger than any other dredge in existence.

"Building a dredge was a complex operation. First, horses and drag lines were employed to dig a dry pond. Timbers were laid out at the deepest point, and the planking bolted on. As soon as the joints were packed with oakum, water was admitted to the pond. Complete with superstructure and machinery, the monster had a weight of 4,070,000 pounds. It required thirty-three carloads of lumber and forty-two carloads of machinery. It could pump twelve thousand gallons of water and dig three hundred and thirty cubic feet of gravel per minute. The buckets were linked into an endless chain, connected with link pins eight inches in diameter.

"The dredge could dig fifty feet deep. It wandered along in a zigzag manner, digging a swath three hundred feet wide, moving ten thousand cubic yards per day. It could make a profit on just three cents' worth of gold per cubic yard! Eight men ran the dredge, while two others drilled test holes to determine the most profitable direction for the dredge to take. The dredges ate up, digested, and re-deposited more than a square mile of land."[33]

Today, along the banks of Alder Creek, remains of these behemoths linger, somehow diminutive in comparison to the days when they rapaciously scarred the land in yet another saga of man's eternal quest for riches.

CHEAP CASH
STORE

OVERLAND
STAGE LINE
LIFORNIA STORE
CLOTHING

Although the Virginia Brewery ceased production many years ago, the thirsty visitor can slake his thirst these days on the better known commercial brands

1. All three accounts are related by Jean Davis in *Shallow Diggin's*, pp. 64-5.
2. *Anaconda Standard*, September 15, 1899.
3. *Ibid.*
4. *Ibid.*
5. *Ibid.*
6. Bits of gold larger than a flake (called dust) and smaller than a nugget.
7. Gold was valued at about $18 an ounce at that time.
8. The alder is a member of the birch family. There are no alders there now. They were burned out by a fire in the gulch on July 13, 1863.
9. This is the generally-accepted account. But it's tempting to agree with historian William S. Greever, who in *The Bonanza West*, p. 218, claims Hughes alone went to Bannack for supplies (it's difficult to imagine after striking gold, the entire party would leave their new finds). Greever continues, "He refused tempting offers to slip back secretly. When he did leave, quite openly, somewhere between three and four hundred men followed him. After traveling awhile stopped and held a meeting. He said the total panned out so far was $189, told what the prospects appeared to be, and then warned that he would go no farther unless the stampeders promised to give each of the six discoverers two hundred feet of ground, rim to rim, claims which would never be jumped or taken away from them. . . . That night, when almost everybody was asleep, Hughes and some of his particular friends stole away at eleven o'clock so that they could stake as close as possible to the discovery. The rest of the stampeders, angry now, arrived on June 6, 1873, in time to get good claims for themselves."
10. The site of the discovery is about a mile from Virginia City. A marker shows the site.
11. Sassman, "Metal Mining in Historic Beaverhead," p. 290. Sassman reports the first stamp mill in Montana was built by William Arnold and J. F. Allen during the winter of 1862-1863. What was probably Montana's first stamp mill was begun at Bannack by blacksmith William S. Arnold in 1862, and was completed by J. F. Allen the following spring.
12. Camps were called shebangs.
13. Dorothy M. Johnson, *Western Badmen*, p. 27. Some authorities, including Toole, indicate there were twenty-four principal members of the gang; Glasscock indicates there were about fifty gang members (p. 30).
14. Plummer had been a marshal in California.
15. Such wayside inns were referred to as a ranch.
16. Thomas J. Dimsdale in *The Vigilantes of Montana*, Oklahoma, 1953, p. 23, implies the road agents must have looked and sounded most fearsome as they used a pair of

Stage productions are held during the summer at the Opera House, while the Bale of Hay Saloon on the left, offers what would be expected of such an establishment

revolvers, a double-barreled shotgun, a knife or dagger and shouted, "throw up your hands, you sons of b — — s!"

17. "Bummer Dan Bar," on the edge of Virginia City, was named after him. A million in gold is said to have come from the bar.
18. Wolle, *Montana Pay Dirt*, p. 26.
19. Others feel the murder of packer and freighter Lloyd Magruder precipitated action to form the vigilance committee. Dimsdale (who spelled the name Tbalt) would seem to indicate no single event was the sole motivating factor.
20. In Chapter 16, *Gold Rushes and Mining Camps of the Early American West*, Fisher describes how it wasn't uncommon for the Vigilantes to give up to 100 lashes, shave heads, and cut off ears of the errant. Apparently those arrested were infrequently beaten to death.
21. Dorothy Johnson, introduction to N. P. Langford's *Vigilante Days and Ways*, Montana State University Press, 1957, p. XXVI.
22. *Hysham Echo,* September 28, 1933.
23. Conical huts made of brush.
24. Years after the hanging, several Vigilantes went to Cemetery Hill and retrieved Lane's club foot. The bones, still in his stocking, are now displayed in a glass bell in the Virginia City Museum.
25. Some say one of the original Vigilantes boiled the flesh of Gallagher's skull and gave it to a Virginia City fraternal organization, where it is still used in secret rites.
26. *Hardin Tribune Herald*, September 19, 1930.
27. *Dillon Daily Tribune*, March 12, 1948.
28. Langford, p. 299.
29. Prostitutes.
30. The Slades lived in a stone tollhouse several miles from Virginia City. Today the house is said to be haunted. Dorothy Johnson, in the introduction to *Vigilante Days and Ways* writes: "Two sheepherders who took shelter there at different times did not live through the night. Some people say that the ghost of Virginia Slade gallops past on her black horse, screaming in the night to try to stop the Vigilantes from hanging her husband." (p. XXXIV)
31. It must have been a costly trip. The fare for the four-day trip was about $225, plus up to $1.50 per pound for baggage. It's unknown whether the body went at "passenger fare" or at the "baggage" rate.
32. Sassman, pp. 294-5.
33. Weis, *Ghost Towns of the Northwest*, pp. 289-90.

YELLOWSTONE COUNTRY:

Scene of Teddy Roosevelt's temporary White House.

Jardine Mining Company's Revenue Mill

Several mining camps were located in the area north of Yellowstone National Park.

Among them—Yellowstone City is gone; the original sites of Nye and Cinnabar have disappeared, although towns of the same names still exist near the original townsites. Other towns in the area—Miner, Carbella, and Sphinx—apparently have vanished. There are scattered, tattered remnants of Independence, Solomon City, Lake City, and Hidden Treasure Bench.

Notable about Cinnabar: it served as America's temporary seat of government for sixteen days in 1903. When President Theodore Roosevelt came to Gardiner to dedicate the northern entrance to Yellowstone Park, arrangements had not been completed to accommodate the temporary White House. So he and his entourage set up headquarters at the Cinnabar railroad station. Presidential Secretary William Loeb, Jr. conducted affairs of state from a string of Pullman and parlor cars from Cinnabar.[1] Messengers communicated with the President as he roamed the area. An official of the Associated Press remarked, "Well . . . this blooming town will be wiped off the map when we leave. It's a mystery to me how it got on it in the first place."[2]

Remains of Independence can still be found, but the road is rough and long; and for most, the trip is not worth the effort.

Cooke City, along with many other towns in the area, was in Indian territory. Chief Joseph of the Nez Perce tribe passed through there in 1877 on an abortive attempt to flee to Canada. Joseph's warriors terrorized the area and burned mills and took silver bullion, which they reportedly cast into bullets; mining operations resumed shortly after their visitation.

Today, Cooke City, even with its interesting mining history and its seven hills of gold, silver, lead and iron (somewhat paralleling the seven hills of Rome), can only be classified as a somewhat gaudy tourist town.

Near Gardiner is Electric,[3] scene of the remains of coke ovens, diminished annually by those who haul away the bricks to make fireplaces. And so, perhaps, the term "brick hunters" should legitimately be added to that of bottle hunters as destroyers of Montana ghost towns.

Electric, founded in 1898 by the Montana Coal and Coke Company, provided power for nearby Aldridge.

Weis, in *Ghost Towns of the Northwest*, gives this account of activities at Electric:

"At Electric, the coal was loaded on small railroad cars and hauled by a dinky (a small locomotive) to the kilns. There were 254 kilns, each hemispherical in shape and about twelve feet in diameter. Railroad tracks ran above and alongside each row of kilns. Bricklayers, most of them Italians, would break open each oven. After cooling, 'pullers' would hook out the coke, and load it on the cars. The masons would then brick up the oven again. Another smaller hole would be broken in the top, six tons of coal poured in, and the oven bricked to seal out the air. Heat from the former batch was enough to ignite the new charge. Seventy-two hours later the conversion was complete, and the process was repeated. Cheaper grades were given thirty-six hours. The coke was shipped by rail to the massive smelters at Anaconda, Montana."[4]

It's interesting to note the effects the dictates of the federal government have had on Montana mining history. Judgments of what constitutes "precious metals" have varied greatly, thus often causing "boom" or "bust" conditions for mining operations. Not only in the Yellowstone area, but elsewhere throughout the state, these listings of strategic metals have ranged from gold, silver, and copper to arsenic and arsenopyrite.[5]

The Revenue mill of the Jardine Mining Company, the company office building, and fire-fighting equipment are speckled amidst buildings which are vestiges of the town which somehow managed to

Livery stable at Emigrant

live, partially because of the needs of the U.S. government for arsenic through World War II.

Also to be found in Jardine are a head-gate shack which had controlled water flow leading to a double waterwheel which provided electricity to the town and its mills.

The Revenue mill held forty stamps, each weighing hundreds of pounds. Each stamp is reported to have dropped ninety times per minute.

An old-timer described the scene this way: "With forty of them stamps going, the sound was more than noise. You could feel it! Felt good, though—felt just like a pay-check on Saturday night."[6]

A popular scene in the ghost town of Jardine is the headstone on the grave of George W. Welcome. The word "Welcome" is printed across the top of the stone. This "town where the cemetery says welcome," was reported in Ripley's "Believe it or Not."[7]

During war time, the effect on mining operations has been marked, as the need for strategic materials has varied. Sometimes mining operations which were marginal or sub-marginal or even closed down become lucrative. Others which had previously been successful were forced to close. Often mining equipment was sold as scrap metal for the war effort —never to be replaced. Mines filled with water, timbers rotted, and because of marginal profit potential, were never reopened; although rich deposits still lie in many areas of the Treasure State.

For example, in Jardine's Mineral Hill, gold reserves are placed at five million dollars.[8]

1. Cinnabar was named for deposits of this principal ore of mercury thought to be in the area.
2. *Silver State Post* (Deer Lodge), June 30, 1938.
3. Sometimes referred to as "Electric City." Originally the settlement was known as Horr, but was changed to Electric or Electric City in 1904 when an electric power plant was installed. Nearby Electric Peak, often struck by lightning, may have influenced the naming of the town.
4. Weis, *Ghost Towns of the Northwest*, pp. 257-9.
5. Arsenopyrite is a principal source of arsenic.
6. Weis, p. 247.
7. *Ibid.*
8. Weis, p. 252.

Jardine's primitive fire fighting equipment

Office of the Jardine Mining Company

Conlin's confectionary at Chico

ZORTMAN:

And how Dutch Louie's hiding from the vigilantes led to the wealth of the Little Rockies.

Zortman lies in the Little Rockies, in northeastern Montana.

In 1868 a party of eight prospectors briefly searched for gold in the area, but not until 1884 did the district attract much attention.

What led up to the 1884 bonanza, during which 2,000 men swarmed to the area, is recounted by old Billy Skillen, the "Sage of Fort Belknap."

"About July fourth," Billy said, "there happened to be some trouble between a white man and a breed at the races over some betting. The white man's name was Rattlesnake. He knocked the breed down, made him apologize and give back the money he had taken. Then the two rode to Reed's Fort in the Judith, or Lewiston, went into the saloon to get a drink, first tying their horses to the rack outside. When they came outside, the citizens thinking they were a tough outfit, which they were, opened fire on them. Rattlesnake and one bystander was killed. From this time on, the 'strangling'[1] of horse thieves and road agents started through northern Montana.

"At this time Dutch Louie[2] ran a ranch on Crooked Creek where these toughs would stop. . . . Suspicion fell on Louie and the 'stranglers' as the vigilantes were called, got after him. So he went into the Little Rockies with Frank Aldrich and Pike Landusky. They prospected for gold and found some in a creek which they named Alder. Frank Aldrich, who was with Pike Landusky and Dutch Louie when gold was discovered, says they were not the first to discover gold in the Little Rockies, as near the mouth of the gulch where they were working was a pit 100 feet long, by 150 feet wide, that had evidently been sluiced out years before. This discovery was made on Beauchamp's creek.

"Quartz was soon found . . . but little real headway was made until . . . the reduction by cyanide. That was when real wealth began to pour out of the Little Rockies. Thus it was through the fact Dutch Louie was hiding out from the vigilantes that the wealth of the Little Rockies was discovered."[3]

Pete Zortman (for whom the town is named) is said by some to have located the Alabama mine. Others say Zortman got the mine third-hand. In any event, by 1893 Zortman and a partner owned the Alabama.

Other mining areas were developed by Charles Whitcomb and B. D. Phillips. Whitcomb and Phillips expanded operations at the Ruby mine, making it the largest cyanide operation in the state. The Little Rockies grew to be the second-largest producer in Montana. Whitcomb procured the Little Ben mine, which between 1935 and 1939 produced $1,500,000 in ore.

The Ruby Gulch mine alone is reported to have produced $5,000,000 in gold.[4] The mine was closed in the 1920s, and shortly thereafter the mill burned down.

Disastrous and nearly-disastrous fires were frequent. In 1936 a forest fire burned to the outskirts of town. It burned 23,000 acres and killed four men. Two days after that fire, a second began near the Little Ben mill. The fire burned toward, but did not quite reach, Zortman. Other fires in 1929 and 1944 brought a fiery end to many of Zortman's original structures. Still, the Ruby Gulch[5] mill operated until 1943, and many Zortmanites stayed on. There are about 175 people there now.

Mr. and Mrs. Ray Holzhey, who own the general store and rent cabins, have many a tale about Zortman. Mrs. Holzhey feels strongly about the differences between people during the early days and now. She says, "miners protected their womenfolk and kids. You had nothing to fear. We never locked anything up. The few fights there were were overly publicized. What fights there were were mostly over mining claims. Today, you're not safe to walk alone; you've got to lock up everything. No, give me the good old days, I felt a lot safer then. There weren't any destructive kids then."[6]

She was interrupted by a phone call. A rancher from Landusky needed some supplies. She got them together, and when the mailman came (in what was referred to as "the stage," although it was a four-wheel-drive vehicle), he took the supplies. He dropped them off at the post office in Landusky, and the rancher paid him a quarter for his trouble.

That's the way it is in Montana.

Zortman, founded by Pete Zortman, one of Pike Landusky's friends

1. Members of the vigilance committees were called "stranglers." Very recently, the Lewiston (Reed's Fort) Vigilantes rose again. The September 5 and 6 issues of *The Missoulian* carried items from the AP indicating they were at odds with two Grass Range youths who wished to stop the installation of a replica of a Minute Man I Missile in the city park. The self-styled "Montana Vigilantes" distributed posters which said, "Wanted, 50 Cowboys with shears and clippers Sept. 5, 1970, to patrol Main Street, Lewiston, Montana." No one showed up.
2. "Dutch" Louie Meyers.
3. Florin, *Ghost Town Treasures*, pp. 87-88.
4. What is claimed to be the world's second largest cyanide mill was erected at the mine.
5. Now known as the Gold Reserve.
6. Thomas J. Dimsdale, educated Englishman, educator, newspaperman, first Montana Superintendent of Public Instruction, who lived and wrote during the territory's growing pains wrote (in *The Vigilantes of Montana*, p. 18), "The mountains . . . may be said to circumscribe and bound the paradise of amiable and energetic women. For their labor they are paid magnificently, and they are treated with a deference and liberality unknown in other climes. There seems to be a law, unwritten but scarcely ever transgressed, which assigns to a virtuous and amiable woman a power for good which she can never hope to attain elsewhere. In his wildest excitement a mountaineer respects a woman, and anything like an insult offered to a lady would be instantly resented, probably with fatal effect by any bystander."
See also, Fisher, *Gold Rushes and Mining Camps*, Chapter 14 for a fairly lengthy treatment on how women were treated in the early American West.

BASIN MONTANA TUNNEL COMPANY
ORE PRODUCTION STATEMENT
MONTH OF JULY, 1935

		Wet Tons
Ore Inventory July 1, 1935:		
Primary Bins:		
Comet		-
Gray Eagle		-
Secondary Bins:		
No. 1 - Gray Eagle		125
No. 2 - Comet		40
No. 3 - Comet		125
Total		290
Additions:		
Comet ore mined during July	2,838	
Gray Eagle ore mined during July	1,287	
Ore from Stock Pile during July:		
Comet	1,122	
Gray Eagle	334	
Ore Purchased during July:		
United Gold Mines Corp.	346	
Other	16	5,943
Total inventory and additions		6,233
Less ore milled during July (mine weights)		5,983
Ore Inventory August 1, 1935		250
Primary Bins:		
Comet	70	
Gray Eagle	--	
Secondary Bins:		
No. 1 - United Gold Mines Corp.	40	
No. 2 - Comet	60	
No. 3 - Gray Eagle	80	
Total	250	
Stock Pile:		
Inventory July 1, 1935		9,907
To bins during July - Comet	1,122	
Gray Eagle	334	1,456
Inventory August 1, 1935		8,451

cc FHM BWS MNS File

BASIN MONTANA TUNNEL COMPANY
ORE PRODUCTION STATEMENT
AUGUST, 1935

		Wet Tons
Ore Inventory August 1, 1935:		
Primary Bins		
Comet		70
Gray Eagle		--
Secondary Bins:		
No. 1 - Outside		40
No. 2 - Comet		60
No. 3 - Gray Eagle		80
Total beginning inventory		250
Additions (except stock pile):		
Comet ore mined in August	4,186	
Gray Eagle ore mined in August	1,734	
Ore Purchased in August:		
United Gold Mines Corp.	250	
Paul Williams	28	6,198
Total inventory and additions		6,448
Less ore milled in August (mine weights)		6,013
Ore inventory September 1, 1935		435
Comet	80	
Gray Eagle	70	
Secondary Bins:		
No. 1 - Comet	90	
No. 2 - Comet	80	
No. 3 - Gray Eagle	115	
Total as above	435	
Stock Pile:		
Inventory August 1, 1935		8,451
To bins in August - Comet	563	
Gray Eagle	158	721
Inventory September 1, 1935		7,730

cc FHM BWS MNS File

BASIN MONTANA TUNNEL COMPANY
ANALYSIS OF MAN LABOR
DECEMBER, 1935

CLASSIFICATION	NOVEMBER	DECEMBER
Gray Eagle Mine:		
Miners	16	16
Engineers	2	2
Compressormen	1	1
Laborers	2	2
Trammers	4	4
Teamsters	1	1
Muckers	-	1
Total Gray Eagle Mine	26	27
Comet Mine:		
Miners	46	45
Engineers	3	3
Laborers	7	7
Station Tenders	3	3
Topmen	1	-
Trammers	3	5
Nippers	1	1
Compressormen	2	2
Electricians	1	1
Blacksmiths	2	2
Carpenters	3	3
Sawyers	1	1
Machinists	1	1
Pumpmen	3	3
Pipemen	1	1
Truck Drivers	1	1
Total Comet Mine	79	79
Comet Mill:		
Operators	7	5
Millmen	3	4
Crushermen	2	2
Laborers	4	4
Assistant Assayers	1	-
Teamsters	1	-
Total Comet Mill	18	15
GRAND TOTAL	123	121

cc WHH FHM File

BASIN MONTANA TUNNEL CO.

GENERAL COST - SEPT. 1936

PAYROLL	- Pumpmen	$ 372.00	
	Teamster	101.06	
	Laborer-Watchman, G.E.	140.12	
	Assayer	25.62	
	Electrician	125.00	
	Time-keeper & Bookkeeper	256.10	
	Supts. & Foreman	323.75	
	Total		$ 1,343.65
SUPPLIES	- Power	$ 347.72	
	Compensation	69.27	
	Soc. Sec. Taxes	46.16	
	Insurance	137.36	
	Property Taxes	96.06	
	Miscellaneous	93.41	
	Total		$ 789.98
	Total September Charges		$ 2,133.63

AAR GS FHM RCS File

BASIN MONTANA TUNNEL COMPANY

GENERAL COST - SEPTEMBER, 1937

MINING		GRAY EAGLE	COMET
Payroll	- Development	$ 258.00	$ 1,027.62
	Mining	718.25	7,642.75
	Miscellaneous	1,036.66	5,451.82
	Supervision	250.00	758.00
	Administration	159.80	1,340.00
	Total	$ 2,422.71	$16,247.19
Supplies	- Development	648.91	258.04
	Mining	321.81	2,368.71
	Miscellaneous	150.40	1,010.77
	Hauling Ore	402.06	--
	Compensation, Insurance, Taxes	288.67	1,750.07
	Power	184.46	1,024.98
	Total	$ 1,996.31	$ 7,312.57
Total Mining		$ 4,419.02	$23,559.76
Dry Tons Ore Produced	- Mining	883.4	5,225.0
	Development	--	34.9
	Total	883.4	5,259.9
MILLING			
Payroll	- Operating		3,062.53
	Supervision		400.30
	Total		3,462.83
Supplies	- Operating		4,718.65
	Power		1,125.00
	Compensation, Royalties, Taxes, Ins.		520.02
	Hauling Conc.		831.80
	Total		$ 7,195.47
Total Milling			10,658.30
Dry Tons Ore Concentrated			6,363.8
Dry Tons Concentrates Produced est.			
	Lead		318.1
	Zinc		226.8
	Iron		807.2
	Total		1,352.1
GRAND TOTAL SEPTEMBER CHARGES			$38,637.08

TOTAL COST - MINING & MILLING - PER TON CONCENTRATED:

January	$ 7.24
February	7.58
March	7.42
April	7.62
May	8.02
June	7.40
July	7.08
August	6.22
September	6.07

cc AAR GS FHM BWS RCS File

BASIN MONTANA TUNNEL CO.

GENERAL COST - APR. 1939

MINING		COMET
Payroll	- Development	$ 1,605.08
	Mining	6,038.80
	Miscellaneous	3,905.69
	Supervision	730.00
	Administration	974.40
	Total	$13,253.97
Supplies	- Development	516.32
	Mining	1,576.13
	Miscellaneous	1,270.68
	Total	$ 3,363.13
Expenses	- Compensation, Insurance & Taxes	1,560.80
	Power	1,073.50
	Total	$ 2,634.30
Total Mining		$19,251.40
	Dry Tons Ore Produced - Mining	4250.5
	Development	842.1
	Total	5092.6
MILLING		
Payroll	- Operating	$ 2,925.60
	Repairs & Maintenance	104.43
	Supervision	335.00
	Total	$ 3,365.03
Supplies	- Operating	5,310.24
	Repairs & Maintenance	186.51
	Total	$ 5,496.75
Expenses	- Compensation, Royalties, Taxes & Ins.	513.34
	Hauling Concentrates	698.99
	Power	927.98
	Total	$ 2,140.31
Total Milling		$11,002.09
Dry Tons Ore Concentrated		5270.8
Dry Tons Concentrates Produced - Estimated		
	Lead	231.3
	Zinc	170.8
	Iron	643.3
	Total	1045.4
Grand Total April Charges		$30,253.49
Total Cost - Mining & Milling - Per Ton Concentrated		$ 5.74

cc AAR GS FHM RCS File

BASIN MONTANA TUNNEL COMPANY

ORE AND CONCENTRATE PRODUCTION - COSTS AND ASSAYS

AUGUST, 1939.

ORE PRODUCTION	Dry Tons	Total Cost	Per Ton	Assays Oz. Au.	Oz. Ag.	%Pb.1/2	%Zn
Comet Mine							
Development Ore	459.9	$ 1,987.15	$4.32	0.104	9.01	4.79	1.64
Stoped Ore	4576.3	17,777.48	3.88	0.098	5.95	2.95	3.49
Total Comet Ore	5036.2	$19,764.63	$3.92	0.098	6.23	3.11	3.32
Custom Ore	14.1			0.100	6.04	2.60	13.75
Total Ore	5050.3			0.098	6.23	3.11	3.35
MILLING							
Comet Ore	4996.7			0.099	6.42	3.14	3.31
Custom Ore	14.1			0.100	6.04	2.60	13.75
Total Ore Milled	5010.8	$ 8,987.39	$1.79	0.099	6.42	3.14	3.34
GRAND TOTAL per dry ton Milled (exclus. N. Y. & Butte Office Exp.)		$28,743.02	$5.74				

August - Dry Tons Concentrates Produced - Estimated

Note: Composite Assays Figured from daily bin sample assays		Produced	Shipped	*Amt. Shipped
	Lead	184.9	207.5	$25,000.00
	Zinc	196.3	189.5	4,900.00
	Iron	559.0	595.0	4,800.00
	Total	940.2	992.0	$34,700.00

*Umpires included

cc AAR GS FHM RCS File

BASIN MONTANA TUNNEL COMPANY

ORE AND CONCENTRATE PRODUCTION - COSTS AND ASSAYS

SEPTEMBER 1939

ORE PRODUCTION	Dry Tons	Total Cost	Per Ton	Assay Oz. Au.	Oz. Ag.	% Pb.	%Zn.
Comet Mine							
Development Ore	851.2	$ 2,610.90	$3.07	0.142	11.55	5.78	2.77
Stopped Ore	3731.9	15,026.69	4.03	0.103	5.66	2.27	2.82
Total Comet Ore	4583.1	$17,637.59	$3.85	0.110	6.75	2.92	2.81
Custom Ore	0						
MILLING							
Comet Ore	4568.1	$ 8,635.49	$1.89	0.111	7.02	3.09	2.82
Custom Ore	0						
GRAND TOTAL per dry ton Milled (Exclus. N. Y. & Butte Off. Exp.		$26,273.08	$5.75				

September - Dry Tons Concentrates (Estimated)

Note: Composite Assays Figured from daily bin sample assays		Produced	Shipped	*Amt. Shipped
	Lead	167.9	167.9	$23,000.00
	Zinc	138.8	145.7	6,000.00
	Iron	638.6	594.3	5,000.00
	Total	945.3	907.9	$34,000.00

*Umpires included.

cc AAR GS FHM RGS File